THE LEADER OF

Revealing the **101** Secrets
of Marvelous Leadership
for the 21st Century

Dr. Kevin D. Gazzara

Dr. Murtuza Ali Lakhani

MLS Publishers

THE LEADER OF OZ
This book is a work of fiction. Resemblance to any entities or people, living or dead, is purely coincidental.

First Published 2008
Second Edition Published 2011
Copyright © 2008, 2011, Dr. Kevin D. Gazzara and Dr. Murtuza Ali Lakhani

Published by MLS Publishers
15001 South 20th Place, Phoenix, AZ 85048
www.magnaleadership.com

Cover design by Marleen Lundy
Back cover photo by Dan Coogan
Printed in the United States of America by Lightening Source Inc.

ISBN 978-0-615-20958-6

To my wife, Lorraine, and my two daughters, Kim and Christine, for their selfless support of my dreams. To my sister Karen, and my parents Theresa and Domenic Gazzara, who taught me one of my greatest life lessons 'Whatever anyone else can do, so can you.'

-Kevin D. Gazzara

To my parents, brothers and sister for their love, example and inspiration, and to Shabana, who is my model of grace, and Mehtaab, the joy of our life.

-Murtuza Ali Lakhani

TABLE OF CONTENTS

Introduction

The best way to teach people is by telling a story.
- Ken Blanchard

It's a twister! In one magical moment, our black-and-white business world has been transformed into a marvelous land of vibrant colors. Everything looks upbeat, more alive. Yet every day we come upon employees that possess brains of straw, have a rusted heart, and lack the nerve, and even worse, those ineffective leaders and wicked managers with bottom line-driven decisions and self-centered motivations. Traveling down the yellow brick road, we miss the memories of the gray home we left behind.

Inspired by the enchanting story of *The Wonderful Wizard of Oz*, this parable is about how each one of us can emerge as a marvelous leader in the bright new land. No crystal ball can reveal the answers for us. Answers can only be found within ourselves.

There are thousands of leadership books out there. We wanted to create one that was fun to read and that employees at every level of an organization could relate to. So, pack your bags and travel along the yellow brick road to discover for yourself the hidden secrets of marvelous leadership. We encourage you to assess your leadership practices using the checklist provided at the end of each chapter!

We hope this book will serve as a navigational blueprint for you to find the wisdom, compassion and courage to return to the land you love. Because at the end of the day, there's no place like home!

Acknowledgments

The authors wish to express their sincerest thanks to Christine Gazzara, Dennis Skinner, Ed Oakley, Helenita Ziegler, Kimberly Gazzara, Lorraine Gazzara, Marleen Lundy, Mehtaab Lakhani, Rod Ibieta, and Shabana Soomar for sharing their unique perspectives, for their reviews, and for their enhancement of this book.

The authors would like to extend an extra special thanks to Marleen Lundy for her wizardry in creating The Leader of OZ book cover and for formatting the book.

How This Book Came to Be

It's strange how the creativity process works. Inspiration comes at the most unusual times and from the most unusual places.

The authors, Kevin Gazzara and Ali Lakhani, have known each other for several years. Initially Kevin acted as a mentor to Ali during his doctoral journey on the topic of cross-cultural leadership for global organizations in the Doctor of Management (DM) Program at University of Phoenix. Through their collaborative relationship, a strong professional bond was developed between them around their shared values and passions for making positive contributions to the field of management and leadership.

In June 2007, they jointly decided to take their completed doctoral research outcomes on cross cultural leadership (CALIBER[tm]) and employee engagement (Task Quotient[tm]) and leave their corporate world of 17 years. Along with another colleague, Marleen Lundy, whom they had worked with for many years designing and implementing management and leadership development programs for a Fortune 100 high-technology company, they formed Magna Leadership Solutions LLC.

While traveling from Sacramento to San Francisco to attend an industry conference, Ali and Kevin undertook a challenge to create a cohesive story that would include the knowledge they had gained from doctoral programs, their extensive professional work experiences that spanned several countries, and their assessment tools expertise. Kevin's Task Quotient^{tm} assessment and other tools, such as DISC and Values provided by Target Training International (TTI), plus Ali's **C**ulturally **A**dapted **L**eadership for **I**nspired **B**usiness **E**xcellence and **R**esults assessment (CALIBER^{tm}) established the foundation for their story. Taking such heavy content, weaving the concepts together, and making it interesting to read presented a formidable challenge.

When faced with such obstacles sometimes it helps to step back and share any and all life experiences. During the discovery process, they found a common thread in the movies they liked. Their favorite story of all time was *The Wonderful Wizard of OZ*, and thus the creative process began on adapting that story into a fun-to-read and engaging business parable, connecting all of their concepts for marvelous leadership.

It is hoped that they have accomplished their objective in this humble endeavor. Either way, it would be wonderful to hear from you.

How to Use This Book

We hope that you will find "The Leader of OZ" amusing as well as insightful in the way of identifying and addressing your management and leadership challenges in the workplace today. As you discover the characters in this book, we encourage you to identify them with people in your own world, and even with yourself. If you read this book with "purpose," and relate yourself to the whirlwind of challenges that Dora encounters and resolves during her odyssey, your journey will be so much more rewarding and enjoyable.

At the close of each chapter you will find a summary of:

☐ Marvelous Leadership Secrets

You can use this checklist to evaluate your own leadership practices by checking the box ☑ if this is a practice that you role model on a consistent basis. This checklist can also be used to evaluate your manager and/or other leaders in your organization. We recommend that you maintain a consistent frame of reference for evaluation so that you can calculate your Marvelous Leadership score at the end of the book.

Enjoy your journey with us to the Land of OZ!

Chapter 1: There's No Place Like Home

Wisdom is built up, small step by small step, from most irrational beginnings.

– Bruno Bettelheim

Dora was out of the door at daybreak, the icy winter air feeling tickly on her skin. The earthy smell of burning cedar wafting from brick chimneys peering above the rooftops was a tacit reminder that her sleepy town was still just opening its eyes. But Dora had been up for hours. Finally, the day she eagerly awaited each year had arrived. It was when she and the rest of the managers at Marvelous Snacks headquarters in Farmden, Kansas saw all their friends and colleagues assembled for the final Business Review Meeting of the year.

Dora T. Gayle had a noble face, an innocent smile and engaging eyes that reflected the generosity for which she was widely known. She saw the best in everyone and spoke kindly to them regardless of their position. Because of these qualities, people were drawn to Dora and liked to be around her. She lived in a small house in the Kansas grasslands with her little Scottish terrier named Rainbo, who was her pride and joy.

The final Business Review Meeting of the year was the event at which the leaders of Marvelous Snacks shared the current state of business along with the vision of the future for their company. To Dora, the most gratifying element was to catch that joyfully fulfilled look on employees' faces when they were

1

recognized for their year of hard work and their bonuses were announced. All twelve hundred employees were in attendance on the factory floor where this meeting took place.

Marvin E. Lewis, the white-haired founder and president of Marvelous Snacks, was dressed in comfortable clothes with a green neckerchief around his collar. He looked as genial, down-to-earth, and approachable as ever. He was affectionately nicknamed Professor Marv by friends because of his passion for experimenting and teaching.

Just that morning, a prominent Kansas newspaper ran a special tributary piece calling Professor Marv the "Edison of the Edibles" marveling at his gift for producing new snack recipes that had led to the 400-fold financial growth of his company over the last thirty years. Hailing him as an outstanding citizen leader, the article included Professor Marv among the "All-Time Great Kansans!"

Professor Marv was equally venerated inside the company for the leadership, optimism and purpose he inspired in all those who wanted to contribute, seeking guidance from him. As he arrived at the podium, the employees quickly stood with a warm and seemingly endless round of applause. After they were seated, Professor Marv took the microphone, "Hope you all enjoyed your breakfast. My crystal ball tells me that you have saved some room for dessert and I am pleased to bring you some delectable news this morning." The Professor was a genius at epigrams, having the habit of quickly cutting to the key message. "As a result of all of your

2

hard work, our company has recorded another 10% growth this year."

The employees broke into applause.

"And in view of our success, I am pleased to announce a 30-day bonus for all employees to be included in your next paychecks." Again, the employees exploded into boisterous ovation.

"This is our 30th consecutive profitable year. We have been successful not only because of our excellent execution but also because we have been willing and able to renew ourselves. Let's reflect on it a moment. During the first Marvelous decade, our primary product was potato chips. During the second we expanded into other snacks and soft drinks, and over this last decade we have grown our line of products and brands into areas such as health foods. I want to share the credit with each one of you. Your work ethic, adaptability and creative energy will allow us to continue to delight our customers *and* keep our promises to our stakeholders in the future.

"I also would like to thank my staff members for their tireless contributions to our continued success: Dora, Hank, Zach, and Hillary." At those words, the employees gave the four managers a special round of applause in acknowledgment of how competently, ingeniously and compassionately they managed their respective organizations.

Dora T. Gayle was the manager of Human Resources, which Professor Marv regarded as the most critical function of a company. He believed Human Resources could only be managed well by a truly good human being. His philosophy was "Put people first and success will follow." He deeply valued Dora in her role.

Of all the functions she had managed at Marvelous over the years, Dora's strongest passion was for Human Resources. She was highly respected in the company and her work was guided by the highest moral values of honesty, fairness, and responsibility. She considered the past eight years of reporting directly to Professor Marv as the most enriching and valuable part of her 30-year career at Marvelous. She had learned immensely from him as he guided her through many twists and turns during the tumultuous times.

Hillary S. Woodsmith led the Design and Manufacturing function at Marvelous Snacks. Her colleagues profoundly admired her creativity and her office was wallpapered with patents and awards showing her cognitive competency. Being somewhat of a tightwad, she was noted for spending the company's money as if it were her own, ensuring that everything was done effectively and efficiently. Hillary had previously worked at a world-class farm machinery manufacturer and over the past year, she had begun implementing the Six Sigma and Lean Production programs in the Marvelous factory. This initiative was paying off handsomely with improved quality and efficiency, along with customer satisfaction.

Zach I. Coward was responsible for leading the Marketing and Sales organization, always thinking of imaginative ways to sell and promote Marvelous products. Although he did not have a college degree, he was one of the smartest and most results-oriented employees in the company. From his vast experience, he had an immense practical understanding of his customers' wants and needs, and how they went about making their buying decisions. He could mix the four Ps—products, price, promotion and place—to maximize the company sales. Zach's organization leveraged the Marvelous brand, up-selling their products on value and image, which helped them achieve even higher margins over their competition. His approach was a critical part of the company's financial success.

Hank C. Straumann managed Finance and Infrastructure operations at Marvelous Snacks. He was meticulous and painstakingly ethical with his numbers which gained him great respect from his coworkers. Everyone trusted him with analyzing how new investments would add value to the company, how product portfolios could be designed to maximize the returns for a given level of risk, and how the company could maintain an optimal level of capital. Unlike some of his counterparts in other companies, Hank had a big heart and found imaginative ways in which the company could contribute to the Farmden community.

As the Business Review Meeting concluded, Dora noticed a grimace on Professor Marv's face that seemed to indicate some discomfort.

"Are you all right, Professor Marv?" Dora inquired.

"Ah, yes...I might have taste-tested too many products this morning. Not to worry, I will be fine," replied Professor Marv, his normally healthy face turning just a shade less pink than normal. "Now let's get back to work, we have a lot of product to move this quarter." Very shortly after the meeting, things got back to normal, the entire Marvelous Snacks operation flowing like a graceful, well-synchronized machine.

Later that afternoon, the weather in Farmden took a wild turn for the worse. East and West winds were blowing ferociously and a terrible twister was rapidly developing. In the midst of this stormy weather, a devastating piece of news reached Dora's desk. Professor Marv had been hospitalized in the ICU! She had been asked to come to the hospital instantly. With a writhing heart and tearful eyes, she headed to Farmden General Hospital as quickly as possible.

Chapter 1 - Marvelous Leadership Secrets

- ☐ **1.** Put people first, results will follow.
- ☐ **2.** Use leadership as the fundamental source of organizational performance, business results, and stakeholder fulfillment.
- ☐ **3.** Make leadership everyone's responsibility, not just of those at the top.
- ☐ **4.** Recognize and reward everyone who contributes to the success.

Chapter 2: The Terrible Twister

Our greatest glory is not in never failing, but in rising up every time we fail.

--Confucius

As the chilling winds whistled through the joints of the hospital doors, Dora waited for the report on Professor Marv. Unexpectedly, one of the windows in the hospital blew open and a cold gust of air filled the room. As Dora quickly closed the window, her mind flashed back to her first conversation with the Professor the day she was hired at Marvelous Snacks.

Dora had been forced to drop out of a local university when her family could no longer afford the tuition. Putting her dream of earning a college degree on hold, she wandered the narrow streets of Farmden looking for a job. Her walk that fortuitous day brought her to the door of a tiny shop, the very first Marvelous Snacks store that had just opened. The sign on the door, "Now Hiring Marvelous People," brought a little smile to her face as she entered the store. Filling out an application, under "Education," Dora wrote, "None. Wish I could afford it."

Professor Marv had looked over her application and said with a smile, "Dora Gayle, your wit suggests you are a smart woman and your honesty tells me you truly need work. I was a student and then a teacher at the very same university you just left. Without my education, I would not have been able to formulate snack recipes and start my own business. I'll hire you on the spot if you accept my very first offering of the Marvelous Education

Scholarship. You will have a job and be able to finish the education you were forced to abandon. Do not let these wild winds blow you off course. Continuing your education is important."

Professor Marv's mysterious kindness had a profound impact on Dora. In an instant, he saved her from straying from her heart's path at a critical time in her life. She immediately felt intensely loyal to him, sensing it was a kindred connection that would last a very long time. Over her thirty years of hard work at Marvelous Snacks, Dora earned the trust and admiration of the Professor. Every day Dora was conscious of the gifts of education, mentorship, and parent-like guidance as blessings from him. She would do anything to help Professor Marv.

Dora was awakened from her flashback by the soothing voice of Dr. Hartley, Kansas' finest cardiologist, as he walked into the waiting room. "Ms. Gayle, I would like to have a private word with you if I may." With a slight bow, he walked Dora out of the waiting room to a spot near the ICU.

"I'm afraid I have some bad news," he said. "The Professor has suffered a heart attack and he will most likely be out of commission for at least the next few weeks. He needs complete bed rest."

Dora's heart sank at those words as an endless stream of thoughts flowed through her mind. She was concerned about the pain the diagnosis would cause Professor Marv, who enjoyed being so active and engaged in his work. She wanted to cry but kept herself together.

The doctor handed Dora an envelope marked, "Urgent and Confidential", and remarked, "Ms. Gayle, the Professor wanted you to read this. He should be ready to see you as soon as we complete his blood work."

As Dora read the single sheet of paper tucked inside the envelope, her eyes glazed over and her jaws trembled with distress. The memo was succinct but a bit cryptic.

Urgent and Confidential

From: Glenda Ozborn, OZborn Technology, Ruby City, CA

To: Dr. Marvin E. Lewis, Marvelous Snacks, Farmden, KS

Subject: 21-Day Escrow and Evaluation

This is to acknowledge the receipt of your signed Letter of Intent for the merger of our two companies.

The funds for the merger have been put into an escrow account and we are ready to facilitate your evaluation during the 21-day cooling-off period.

We look forward to hearing from you regarding your next step.

Sincerely yours,

Glenda Ozborn, Ph.D.

Merger? Escrow? Evaluation? A thousand more questions entered Dora's mind as she said quietly to herself, "Looks like my world is about to be turned upside down!" She knew that this would be the most important conversation she had ever had with the Professor.

In the meantime, Zack, Hank and Hillary arrived in the waiting room. "Thank you for coming," Dora said, noting the visible concern on their faces. "Professor Marv suffered a heart attack, and the doctor just told me it will be a few weeks before we know if he'll be out of the woods. We are his only family, and he is going to need our support and prayers."

Hillary said, "Dora, you are the closest to the Professor. Just let us know what needs to be done, and we'll do it." Each of them hugged Dora. She felt fortunate to be in the company of such caring people she could truly count on.

A nurse arrived in the waiting room and said, "Ms. Gayle, Professor Marv is ready to see you." Hillary, Zach and Hank stayed in the waiting room to get the report on the Professor's health when Dora returned from the ICU. Entering Professor Marv's room, she found him in a bed surrounded by a dozen monitoring devices and connected to an intravenous system. It tore Dora's heart to find the Professor in that position. She walked up and gently held his hand. "Professor, how do you feel?" she inquired. "We have been worried about you."

He remarked, "I feel A-OK. After a lifetime of avoiding sick days from work, it feels like time to take a vacation. Knowing that I have you with me lets me rest a bit easier."

"Your health is very important to all of us and we want you to get well very soon," Dora replied. Suddenly getting serious, Professor Marv said, "Dora, did you look at the memo?" Dora nodded. "The time for a fundamental change is here. We are reaching a turning point in the life of Marvelous Snacks. I have been reflecting and making some plans to move the company forward and build new alliances in order to make the foundation of our company even stronger for the foreseeable future."

Dora listened intently as Professor Marv continued, "There are some concerns on the horizon. Big snack-food companies are on an eating binge, gobbling up smaller successful businesses like ours. They have spread their distribution wings into the online space leveraging their significant capital and brands. We have ignored that avenue in the past.

"As you may have gleaned from the memo, I have been having some confidential talks with an old friend of mine from college who now works in California. Her company, OZborn, known in the industry simply as "OZ," provides technology for online distribution of products. She has hired very capable people but has had only moderate success. OZ needs a company like Marvelous to use its technology and Marvelous needs a company like OZ to enter the land of e-commerce. There appears to be a potential for some excellent synergy between our two firms. Dora, I am asking you to go to Ruby City, travel to OZ, and see if there is a match."

"I appreciate your trust in me very much, Professor," Dora said with complete sincerity. "What would you like to see happen?"

"Our first goal is to evaluate the feasibility of a merger with OZ. I continue to believe that 'if you put people first, success will follow.' Our primary focus for the evaluation therefore is to ensure that the cultural personalities of our companies and respective people are compatible. Glenda is a dear friend, and you are the best HR professional around. You know how to help people perform to their true potential. I want Glenda to be successful. So while you are at OZ, take any opportunity you have to use your organizational development magic as you have at Marvelous Snacks. The best way to see if there is a fit between her staff and ours is to try to initiate change. If it can't take hold in a few weeks you will know that there is little chance of success in the long run."

Suddenly, the nurse knocked on the door and announced that it was time for Dora to leave the Professor, for he needed his next round of tests and his rest.

"There is little time to waste, Dora. We have fewer than 21 days for our decision. As much as I know that you would like to be by my side at this time, I would like you to fly out to Ruby City on the first available flight. The future of our company rests on your shoulders."

Strengthened and inspired by the Professor's trust and encouragement, Dora's desire to make his mission come true was pushed to the top of her priority list. The next several weeks would require her to use everything that she had learned from the Professor to help navigate the Marvelous ship through unchartered waters.

Chapter 2 - Marvelous Leadership Secrets

☐ **5.** Recognize that success is neither permanent, nor a chance occurrence.

☐ **6.** Empower and grow people's capabilities — get them to step out of their comfort zone.

☐ **7.** Scan internal and external environments continuously to fine tune the direction of the organization.

☐ **8.** Continuously develop new leaders who can succeed you.

☐ **9.** Initiate bold strategies to transform and align the organization with the changing environment.

THE LEADER OF OZ

Chapter 3: We Are Not In Kansas Anymore

You do not lead by hitting people over the head—that's
assault, not leadership.
– Dwight D. Eisenhower

As Dora boarded the airplane, the flight attendant offered her a newspaper and the headline "Earthquake Shakes Ruby City" caught her eye. During her three-hour flight from Kansas, Dora made notes on the local news in Ruby City and on the OZborn Technology's history. Dozens of intriguing questions cropped up in her mind. Why had OZ fallen off the list of the most promising small companies in the last two years? What was Glenda, OZ's spirited CEO pictured in the Kismet magazine, really like? Why had Professor Marv picked OZ for the merger?

Dora's plane landed with a thud rousing her from her deep thoughts. Rainbo was snugly nestled in his pet carrier under the seat in front of Dora and woke up with a little woof. Before leaving Kansas, Dora discovered that OZ had a policy that allowed pets in the workplace. Not wanting to burden anyone with the terrier's care, she decided to bring him along for the adventure.

During the walk from the gate to the baggage claim area, Rainbo pranced around in his sparkly rhinestone collar wagging his tail, looking inquisitively at the new faces and glaring lights. He wore a bedazzled look that plainly said, "We're not in Kansas anymore."

As Dora collected her baggage from the carousel, a sweet voice inquired, "Dora Gayle?" As she turned, she saw this perfect woman with glistening hair, shining eyes and an amazing figure. Unmistakably, it was Glenda! "Glad you made it safely; I have been so looking forward to meeting you."

"So have I," said Dora, a bit shaken by Glenda's appearance. "It's so nice of you to come in person. Actually, I was expecting the HR director, Eve Eastwick, to meet me."

"I will tell you that unfortunate story later, but first, tell me how Professor Marv is doing. I have been so concerned about him," said Glenda with utmost sincerity.

"I am afraid no one's sure. They are still running more tests. We should know in a few weeks' time," said Dora in a sorrowful voice.

"We'll hope and pray for the best," answered Glenda. "The Professor has produced many miracles in his life for others. It may be time for him to receive a miracle of his own."

Glenda, Dora and Rainbo boarded the limousine waiting just outside the baggage claim area. "That's an adorable pet you have," Glenda said.

"Thanks. This is Rainbo. When I read that you have a pets-allowed policy at OZ, I decided to bring him along," replied Dora with gratitude.

"We want our employees to feel at home, so I am very glad you brought a little bit of Kansas with you," Glenda replied with a smile.

After a brief silence, Glenda, with a quiet look of seriousness, said, "The Professor has told me quite a bit about you, Dora. He holds you in the highest esteem and, knowing the Professor as I do, I am sure you really are wonderful. This job ahead of us is truly critical to the health of both of our companies. I am pleased to entrust you to evaluate this proposed merger and help us make the right decisions. I love OZ and its people with all my heart, and I want only the best for them and for our company. I do have to admit that my preoccupation with other ventures over the past two years has taken its toll on the performance and results at OZ. I hope your assessment from an outsider's perspective over the next three weeks will help provide us with objective and unbiased inputs." Dora sensed that there was a hidden message in Glenda's last statement.

Glenda continued, "Let me tell you about a couple of recent important developments. I am very sorry to say that Eve was one of the casualties of yesterday's earthquake. She had been working for over a year on renovating an historic farmhouse on the eastside hills and was at the site for a final inspection when the quake hit. The original structure collapsed on top of her, killing her instantly."

"Oh my, I am so sorry to hear that. Did she have a family?" said Dora in shock.

"Eve was somewhat of a recluse, and had no family other than some unique pet birds and even bats that resided in her barn. I will be busy the most of today taking care of her final arrangements. I really am glad to have you here during this time. We need to get on the road to reach our destination on time."

With a solemn look, Glenda pulled out a laptop computer from her briefcase with the ruby red OZ logo emblazoned on the front. She handed it to Dora and said, "This was retrieved from Eve's house. It may have information that you might be interested in. It's still set to Eve's login ID, "eve.l.eastwick" and her password, "OZ4ME". Guard the laptop with your life and never let it out of your sight."

Dora felt a bit uneasy about using Eve's login and password, but nodded and carefully tucked the laptop away in her briefcase as Rainbo watched her attentively.

Their limo pulled up to the yellow brick walkway in front of a group of tall structures bearing the name, OZborn Technology. All of the buildings were white and uniformly colored in emerald green stripes. Once inside, Dora and Rainbo received their badges. They then took the elevator to the third floor.

"I will introduce you to Mitchell, our Finance Manager. Since Eve's departure, he has volunteered to also act as the manager of Human Resources. My other three staff members are Cher Crowe, who manages Information Technology; Tim Mann, who manages Design and Development; and Howard Lee Lyon, who manages Sales and Marketing. Oh, speaking of the devil, I see that Mitchell is in his office right now."

Mitchell Westfall was a tall balding man with a head the size of a watermelon. He had protruding eyes and a face that wore a sinisterly feeble smile exposing his tobacco-stained teeth. Sitting beside him was his pet, a small monkey named Wingo. At the sight of Glenda and Dora, Mitchell casually rose from his chair, as if he were expecting them.

Glenda handled the introductions, "Mitchell, this is Dora Gayle from Marvelous Snacks. I'd like to ask you two to carry on from here. Once you are finished, Mitchell, please introduce Dora to Cher, Tim, and Howard."

Turning to Dora, Glenda continued, "I will be available for you at any time, here's my cell phone number, just give me a call whenever you need me, all right? Good luck." With that, Glenda walked back toward the elevator, leaving Dora and Mitchell alone, face to face.

Mitchell grabbed his pet, started walking from his office, and ordered Dora to follow him. Dora felt a bit hesitant but she continued after him into a spacious, luxuriously equipped conference room with a sign on the door, "Reserved for Mitchell D. Westfall and Eve L. Eastwick."

"Well Ms. Gayle, I know what mission brings you here, but allow me to caution you about a few things." Just as he finished speaking, the monkey snapped at Rainbo. "Wingo, stay!" shouted Mitchell as he pulled out a long wooden pencil from his pocket and flicked it at the poor creature. The shocked monkey scurried backward to avoid being struck.

Lighting a cigar blatantly in violation of the company nonsmoking policy he continued, "People around here, Ms. Gayle, are like this monkey. They will not behave unless they are monitored, kept in line, and punished accordingly. I keep him around because he reminds me of people and their behaviors." Dora sat there silently in disbelief at what she was seeing and hearing. She was concerned for the monkey, but he had sprung back up as if accustomed to Mitchell's treatment.

Mitchell continued, "Has Glenda given you anything that belonged to Eve?" Dora mentioned the laptop. Immediately, Mitchell became impatient and demanded that Dora give it to him.

Dora replied, "Glenda gave it to me in confidence and I am committed to not let it out of my sight."

Mitchell shook his pencil at Dora and Rainbo, "Fine, but that laptop is of no use to you. You won't know how to make sense of the data. Remember that I am the manager of the Human Resources and Finance departments and you need me. Our paths will cross soon, and I'll deal with you at that time." With that, Mitchell roughly picked up his monkey and quickly left the conference room leaving only a puff of cigar smoke behind.

With Rainbo watching her, Dora sat there stunned. "That was unbelievable. It appears as if the next three weeks will be intense. I sure hope we survive this trip!"

Chapter 3 - Marvelous Leadership Secrets

☐ **10.** Ensure that your leadership is defined by values, behaviors, and deeds—not simply by words and personality.

☐ **11.** Empower people based on their ability and willingness.

☐ **12.** Stand up for what you believe in, even under the fiercest threats.

☐ **13.** Recognize that selflessness, sensitivity and humility are foundational traits of a leader.

☐ **14.** Build an environment in which leaders and followers interact as equals.

THE LEADER OF OZ

Chapter 4: Follow the Yellow Brick Road

The meeting of two personalities is like the contact of two chemical substances: if there is any reaction, both are transformed.

– C.G. Jung

"Rainbo, I can hardly believe what just happened!" whispered a bewildered Dora. "I'm not quite sure where to start. I think it's time for us to take a walk."

Dora left the conference room and headed downstairs to the cafeteria for lunch. Her mind was racing with ideas as she walked around the building to get acquainted with the surroundings. Later, as she approached a grassy area in the open courtyard, she noticed Glenda reviewing a colorful slide presentation, sitting at one of the tables with her cat named Munchkin.

"Hello, Glenda. I was wondering if you would have some time today to discuss some ideas I am pondering," Dora asked with a hopeful tone.

"No time like the present," responded Glenda, catching Dora by surprise. "You've got to have priorities. The merger is #1 priority on my list, so anything you need trumps what I am working on right now."

"Thank you, but I haven't had the time to prepare a nice presentation like the one you are reviewing," Dora said.

"Forget it. I am finding that we are spending far too much time preparing jazzy presentations and not enough time doing real work. Look at this," said Glenda as she handed Dora the cover page and pointed to the lower left corner with the notation, 'Revision 7.' Dora was encouraged by the fact that Glenda preferred substance over style.

Pushing aside the presentation document, Glenda continued, "Give me your thoughts. I've spent the entire morning talking and reading and would enjoy listening for a while."

"Let me try and paint the whole picture for you, and then I'd like your reaction," Dora said.

"This is the first time I've been involved in evaluating a merger. The process doesn't seem a whole lot different than the yearly assessment of our Marvelous managers, leaders and organizations. The essential elements to such an assessment include the roadmap, the method, and the success criteria. We need to cover all of these during my time here. I plan to use this approach for the evaluation for the merger.

"I remember when Marvelous did its first expansion beyond potato chips. We tried to figure out everything ourselves. That was an unsettling experience since we were putting our time and resources in the wrong areas by inadequately staffing our organizations and underfunding key initiatives. It wasn't a marvelous time for Marvelous, but none of those lessons could have been gleaned from a hundred different management books. One of our key lessons was that we couldn't always make the giant leap forward by only using internal knowledge. Seeking out experts who had done it before helped us ensure we were choosing the right roads to success.

"To get unstuck from our sticky situation we hired this short, little retired management consultant with a big handlebar mustache who had worked for Lollipop Confectionaries. His name was John D. Mayor. He was wonderful! We called him, The Mayor, since he gave us the keys to a new land of sweet opportunity to expand our business.

"The Mayor always said, 'You won't know where you're going if you don't know where you are.' We were trying to do everything one snack at a time, and he made us realize that we needed to pick our strategy and create a blueprint of what success looked like. Coupled with Professor Marv's 'people first' approach, The Mayor gave us a good roadmap of the work ahead. Once we had all the information, we were able to accelerate our expansion to completion in just a few short weeks. I'm confident that this approach can be used over the next two-plus weeks. Am I making sense?"

Glenda nodded, "Go on. What did you do next?"

"Well, The Mayor had a simple formula captured by the acronym, ALAS, which consisted of four steps: 1) Assess, 2) Link, 3) Apply, and 4) Structure. He always told us that if we didn't carry out all four steps, *alas* we'd be stuck back in the same rut!

"It's always best to start at the beginning, Step #1--Assess. We began by having our managers take a leadership inventory, not just the typical 360-degree feedback survey but a true assessment to evaluate their competencies directly in relation to the organizational and business results. With our past methods, we are shooting in the dark, not knowing whether we were getting any real value out of our measurements. The Mayor's methods tied the leadership competencies directly to organizational performance and business results, and he was dead on!"

Glenda jumped into the conversation, "That sounds promising. We do many assessments here as well, but you are right, we never can tell if we'll get any improvement. It's frustrating, but we've never been sure how to verify the cause and effect relationships."

Dora smiled and jumped back in, "We had the same problem. When we were small, it was easy for everyone to communicate with everyone else, so our informal feedback process worked well. However as we grew, the informal system stopped being effective and we turned to the 'spray and pray approach,' spraying lots of training on people and praying that it would work. The inconsistent results indicated that either we weren't spraying sufficiently enough or we weren't praying hard enough," Dora said with her hands clasped. Glenda smiled.

"That's when we recognized the need for Step #2--Link. We had good systems that worked well independently but not together. In addition, it wasn't just about linking different systems as much as it was about having each system be self-monitoring and designed to seamlessly connect to the other systems.

"We realized that HR was actually perpetrating the dysfunction. We were off adding lots of measurements like organizational health surveys and team well-being evaluations, which we never really used. This frustrated the employees and managers even more. The Mayor's approach was that no program or assessment was to be implemented unless it had its own measurement embedded in it. In addition, it had to be tied to organizational objectives. This completely changed the mindset of the whole company, even though it didn't seem that way at first. It took extra time to think through the linkages between the inputs and outputs, and the results were spectacular!" Dora proudly exclaimed.

"Assessing and linking were the first two steps. Step #3--Apply. This step was to implement what we learned on the job and make it part of our Marvelous DNA. We made sure that we had regular feedback to let each of us know if we were straying from the right path. The key was not to have to take extra HR surveys or add more time to do the tracking than the time it took to do the actual task. When you over-engineer a system, creeping elegance takes over and you tend to forget what the real purpose of the system was in the first place."

"I'm an engineer, you know...." Glenda said jokingly. "I know just what you are talking about, since I get that feedback from my staff all the time. Alas! How does the "S" for Structure fit in?" she asked.

"The final step, Step #4--Structure. This part of the process was to ensure that the structures for organization, communication, and evaluation were in place. That way people worked together as a cohesive unit and could be held accountable.

"The Mayor pointed out a particular problem in our reward structure. Before ALAS, individuals and managers were rewarded only for their standalone performance. There were never any rewards for building great teams or for promoting collaboration. We learned that what gets measured gets rewarded, and what gets rewarded gets done. Once managers realized that their bonuses would be tied to their effectiveness in bringing people together to form cooperative relationships, we had a Marvelous transformation."

Glenda thought for a moment and remarked, "As you begin meeting with my staff members, you may be hearing some of the same comments you heard from The Mayor when he assessed Marvelous in the early days. The ALAS process sounds interesting. How did it help with your expansion, and how do you see applying it to your OZ merger analysis?"

"Good questions. First, after we implemented ALAS we discovered we actually had the correct expansion strategy, all the right people, and the appropriate number of resources. We just needed to get them working together as a single unit. As for my merger analysis, I'll score each of the four ALAS steps on a scale from 1 to 5 for completeness to see how OZ compares to Marvelous. The score for Marvelous was not perfect even after we implemented ALAS.

But since I was involved in the successful expansion for Marvelous, I know what our score was when The Mayor first arrived. If OZ's score comes close to the Marvelous score, we'll know that we've got the foundation for the merger to be successful," Dora concluded.

With that closing remark, Dora wrote a number down on a piece of paper and folded it several times. "Here Glenda, take this, it was The Mayor's ALAS score before Marvelous' expansion. We'll open it together at the end of my time here to see where we stand."

Glenda placed the paper in a zippered pouch in her purse and replied, "It will stay here for safe keeping. I'll be anxious to open it to see how close we are."

Dora glanced at her watch "Oh my, it's almost 5:00 PM, I have a series of meetings with your staff members tomorrow, and there's still a lot of preparation to do. Thanks for your time Glenda. This has truly helped me pull my thoughts together. Sorry for interrupting your slide review."

Gently getting her things together, Dora said, "Come Rainbo, let's make our way to the hotel to get checked in."

Chapter 4 - Marvelous Leadership Secrets

☐ **15.** Seek out the experts that have done the work before.

☐ **16.** Assess your leaders as early as possible using tools that do not measure leadership in isolation.

☐ **17.** Apply your learning's immediately to make changes quickly.

☐ **18.** Keep the feedback system simple so that everyone can know how they are doing.

Chapter 5: The Last Straw

Leaders don't create followers, they create more leaders.

– Tom Peters

BANG! WHAM! BASH! DOINK! SMASH! Cher Crowe was rather livid that morning and it was the ball that was paying the penalty as she thrashed it in the squash court. As on most Wednesday mornings, Cher could be found at the local gym a few hours before work. In her mind, she replayed the words of Eve and Mitchell from the previous week. "We have decided to cut your request for IT infrastructure budget by 70%." Yet again, the months of effort put in by her team had been in utter vain.

The team had collected project inputs, performed careful top-down and bottom-up analyses, and diligently scrubbed the numbers before submission, only to find that their recommendations were arbitrarily judged down. The budget that was approved was barely enough to maintain the dated infrastructure that was falling apart quickly.

Cher knew all too well that one of the reasons why OZ was losing its competitive edge was its near-obsolete infrastructure. Even though the older infrastructure doubled the support workload and there was no staffing relief, there were key deserving people in her organization were passed up for raises and promotions. Despite their blood, sweat, and sacrifices for the company the budget just wasn't there, only due to lack of support from Eve and Mitchell. Cher's academic background was limited.

As soon as she had completed high school, her parents forced her to work to help support the family. She always regretted her lack of education, but what she lacked in academic learning she made up for by gaining valuable practical experience on the job and outside, immersing herself in her work with untiring energy. She entertained the highest respect for those who had more formal training than she did. Eve and Mitchell had used Cher's lack of a college education to overrule her on the most important decisions that had a direct impact on her organization.

Snarly-haired, meek-figured Cher was now determined to bring about a change. She needed to be in a place where her ideas would be appreciated and respected. Just as she was contemplating change, the news reached her of Eve's unfortunate accident and the fact that Dora had arrived in town. Strangely, a glimmer of hope arose in her. She jumped into the shower to get ready for work.

As Cher was getting ready, Dora was in her hotel room, carefully reviewing the information she had compiled on Cher's Information Technology organization. She found that this group was experiencing an unusually high turnover. As in a revolving door, people had been hired, trained, and replaced. She also found that the workload had significantly increased in Cher's organization, yet there was very little change in staffing levels.

The organizational health survey results that she found on Eve's laptop revealed that people were discontented and unmotivated. Nearly 60% of the people responded that they would leave their jobs if they had an equivalent alternative. Dora wondered if these results were ever shared with the employees or even with Glenda.

As she continued exploring the laptop contents, Dora became somewhat suspicious of Eve and Mitchell's activities, although the full picture had not yet emerged for her. With her interest piqued, Dora looked forward to her meeting with Cher that morning.

As Dora walked into the OZ building, she noticed some commotion in the hallway. There were small groups of employees gathered, giggling, humming, and smiling. Everyone seemed to be having a good time with ice cream cones being passed around. Not sure what this celebration was about, Dora decided to continue to the conference room for the meeting with Cher. She was alone as she set up Eve's laptop to have the data ready.

Cher walked into the conference room and found Dora waiting for her. "You must be Dora. Pleased to meet you," remarked Cher.

"Likewise, Cher, I have been so looking forward to speaking with you," responded Dora genially. To break the ice, Dora asked Cher if she knew anything about the small festive gathering she had noticed, and she was intrigued by Cher's answer.

"You may find this a bit morbid and tasteless, but the little celebration was related to Eve-L's departure," answered Cher. "I am referring to Eve Eastwick, our HR manager. The employees referred to her as 'Eve-L' or the 'Wicked VP of the East' because of her evil personality. Needless to say, she was not well liked around here. She punished people who spoke up against her HR policies, withheld budgets for training and development, interfered in people's decision making, etc."

Cher continued, "The shocking news is that Witchell—sorry, Mitchell—is covering for her. Employees see Mitchell Westfall as the 'Wicked VP of the West,' being cut from the same cloth as Eve-L, so there is little hope for change at OZ."

Not having the full picture yet in her mind, Dora did not want to prejudge the situation. She nodded, and decided to move on to a more substantial and purposeful topic.

In confidence Dora shared the objectives of her trip with Cher. After attentively listening, Cher opened up, "I would be more than happy to help in any way you need."

Dora replied, "Great. So, let's start with a discussion about your organization. My boss, Professor Marv always says to put people first. Tell me about your people, what they aspire to achieve, what is working, and what is not working in your organization."

The adrenaline from this morning's squash game coursed through Cher's veins as she began opening up to Dora, whom she saw not only as sincere and trustworthy, but also as a person who gave her hope.

"Overall, my organization has great people and processes in place. Our main concern for years has been that we are not included in decision-making. None of our input is taken seriously. Decisions made by Eve-L and Witchell are completely capricious. The result is that no one thinks anymore, as no one considers it worth their while. We have mechanistic jobs, which we perform like machines. It is clear that the innovation and competitiveness of our company has suffered. The inputs we provided on the employee survey have been getting ignored quarter after quarter. If something doesn't change, the remaining good people will be forced to leave OZ," Cher said.

The conference room door sprung open, and one of Cher's employees, Keshava S. Rao, rushed in. Panting, he spoke in an Indian accent, "Cher, sorry to barge in, but the servers have caught on fire. We need you in the Server Room right away." Cher took leave of Dora and rushed out with her employee.

Completely astonished, Dora sat alone in the conference room wondering whether this was a sporadic incident or a predictable one, and how people felt like coming to work in an environment where they were clearly not trusted or empowered. As some of these thoughts were crossing her mind, the conference room door flung open again, and to Dora's complete surprise, Mitchell walked in.

"Meeting interrupted, eh?" Mitchell said, with an evil grin. "Look Miss, I need to have Eve's laptop right now. You give it to me and some of the roadblocks you have been encountering around here may get cleared up."

"I am in no position to give you the laptop," Dora responded firmly. "Your head still appears to be over the rainbow in Kansas. We'll see how your mission goes around here. If I were you, Missy, I would watch my back." With that comment, Mitchell exhaled a thick puff of smoke from his cigar and disappeared into the maze of cubicles.

Chapter 5 - Marvelous Leadership Secrets

☐ 19. Spark the creativity of workers by minimizing mechanistic jobs.

☐ 20. Set high expectations for the employees to achieve maximum output.

☐ 21. Trust people, consider their inputs, and show appreciation for their efforts.

☐ 22. Provide full control of the necessary resources to people to help them get their jobs done well.

☐ 23. Delegate decision making to the lowest level possible in the organization.

Chapter 6: Stuffing the Straw Back Together

Treat people as if they were what they ought to be and you help them become what they are capable of becoming.
— Johann Wolfgang von Goethe

"Come along, Rainbo," Dora said, still a little shaken from the fire incident and Mitchell's veiled threats. "Our journey has truly begun. Now we will have to find our way through this labyrinth."

Dora spent the next two hours completing her review of the IT organization information on Eve's laptop. Expecting that Cher was not returning to the conference room, Dora neatly tucked away the laptop into her briefcase and was ready to get back to Eve-L's vacant office. Just as she was about to leave the conference room with Rainbo, she saw Cher walking down the hall toward her.

"Are things OK?" inquired Dora.

"Everything is back up and running, though we are not sure what caused the fire," responded Cher. "Our IT infrastructure is terribly outdated, and held together by straws. Some of the older chips in the servers heat up badly. Employees joke that we could cook marshmallows over the servers. My solutions team is looking into the root cause of the fire."

"Outdated IT infrastructure?" Dora asked curiously. "I thought technology was OZ's strong suit. How can an online distribution company manage without effective and up-to-date infrastructure?"

"Good question, I can give you my two cents. Do you want to continue our discussion where we left off? If you would like, we can get a cup of cappuccino in the café and continue there." Dora agreed, and they started walking with Rainbo trotting along a few steps behind them.

Dora and Cher got cups of coffee for themselves and a biscuit for Rainbo. They settled down in a quiet corner of the café and Cher started, "Our competitors have created a set of finely tuned business processes and information systems that simultaneously promote agility, efficiency and quality. This allows them to respond instantly to customers and to the changes in the marketplace. I am saddened and frustrated to see OZ fall off the leading edge with each passing day."

Cher took a sip from her cup, and continued, "While other businesses are investing in technology and optimizing their value chains continuously, we have made technology our main Achilles' heel. Older technology is restricting the productivity of our people, increasing downtime and the support load, and undermining our ability to derive full business value."

Very interested in what Cher was saying, Dora inquired, "What would you do differently?"

Suddenly energized by the fact that someone was genuinely attentive to her inputs, Cher answered, "The job of my organization is to maintain the hardware, software, data storage, and networks that comprise the IT infrastructure at OZ. First, I would replace the existing 10-year-old infrastructure with cutting edge technology. I would deploy enterprise-level applications for the management of our supply chain, customer relationships, and knowledge repository. This would support the organization-wide coordination and integration so that the entire company could operate more effectively and efficiently."

Pausing for a moment, Cher continued, "If used properly, IT can be a big value-adding entity for acquiring, transforming and distributing information to improve management decision making, enhancing organizational performance, and ultimately, increasing the firm's profitability."

Dora noted the enthusiasm, energy and drive in Cher's voice, and added, "I agree with you on the value IT brings. I do believe that leadership, business strategy, operations, and IT go very much hand in hand." Using Professor Marv's questioning approach, Dora continued, "So what do you believe is stopping you and others from achieving what is needed for OZ?"

Cher chuckled as she almost spilled her coffee and said, "Well, where do I begin? Let me tell you what happened with our most recent budget request. My team spent months compiling the most urgent project requirements. To our shock and disbelief, this budget was chopped down by 70% of what we requested, a completely arbitrary call by the so-called 'decision makers.' But this is not the first time such a thing has happened around here. Every year we do months of work and then Eve-L and Witchell look at how much we got last year and they give us at least 10 percent less. You can see at this rate I'll be running the entire operation by myself, probably reporting to Witchell's monkey."

"I'm surprised," said Dora, "From my discussions so far with Glenda, she appears to be a very capable and judicious leader. She has been so successful founding this company that I am mystified that you wouldn't be able to talk openly or reason with her."

Cher stood up and started her soft emotional plea, "Glenda's not the problem, and when I said the so-called decision makers, I didn't imply that Glenda was in that group. She is a wonderful participative leader, sometimes to a fault. We have our staff and budget meetings like clockwork every month and many decisions are tabled at the meeting. We all get to present our positions and people listen intently. I think my position bears a little less weight, since I am the one on the staff with the least amount of brains, not having a college degree. That's what Eve-L and Witchell insinuate. Then some witchcraft happens outside of the meeting and decisions you thought would be made in your favor somehow are transformed. The excuse lately has been that we need the money for more important 'strategic' programs. When I continually ask how we will know when we've cut too deep, Witchell tells us 'when something seriously breaks down.' Well people are breaking down."

Dora asked for a copy of Cher's proposed budget from her. They walked back to Cher's office where Dora spent time carefully going through it. They continued their healthy exchange for another two hours while Dora made several notes.

With the energized look that continued enlightenment brings, Dora remarked, "It is clear to me that the competence of your organization is suffering due to both internal and external forces. From my limited analysis, I have five observations. Cher, feel free to tell me if I am wrong or if you don't agree. It looks like:

1. You are struggling to properly plan, fund, and staff the full needs of your organization.

2. People are having a hard time obtaining the resources they need to do their jobs.

3. There is minimal alignment between the goals of your organization and those of OZ.

4. Some autocratic managers are impeding your ability to constructively confront and solve problems.

5. The lack of resources is making it difficult for you to make and meet commitments."

Dora's words soothed Cher's grated nerves. She had always known the problems but the articulation by Dora gave those problems an eloquent form and structure. "No disagreement here," said Cher with her eyes brightening.

Dora responded, "Well then, over the next few weeks, I will be working to analyze the situation at OZ more carefully. Cher, would you like to come along with me on this journey of discovery?"

Instantly, Cher replied, "Yes!"

For the past two years, she had felt that her head was stuffed with straw, as others made the most

important decisions for her organization. Now she saw
that a light bulb was beginning to glow brightly!

Chapter 6 - Marvelous Leadership Secrets

☐ **24.** Properly plan, fund, staff, and manage
projects.

☐ **25.** Make it easy for your followers to secure,
control, and manage the resources for
success.

☐ **26.** Quickly confront and solve complex
problems.

☐ **27.** Align the goals of the departments to support
the mission of the organization.

☐ **28.** Make and meet commitments.

Chapter 7: A Well-Oiled Machine

Leadership, like swimming, cannot be learned by reading about it.
— Henry Mintzberg

As Tim entered the room, he saw Dora staring intensely at her laptop. "Hello," he said, startling Dora. "We do have a meeting at this time, don't we?" Dora quickly stood up to greet him, "Yes, of course, please sit down."

Glenda had told Dora about Tim Mann, the manager of Engineering Design and Development. A thin man, he was a soccer player with lots of enthusiasm. His true passion was for anything dealing with team sports. But more importantly, he loved to do charity work. He was always starting up new employee groups to support some cause by raising money or getting employees to donate their time. Dora now recognized Tim from a funny flyer she had seen on a bulletin board by the OZ cafeteria. He was dressed in a shiny suit of armor holding a lance with some type of trash stuck on the end. It read:

"Don't waste your Sunday watching Football all knight, help us clean up the fairgrounds at the Renaissance festival this weekend. All of the money raised will go to the Ruby City homeless shelter."

Tim had been with OZ since it had started. He was a Stanford graduate in computer science and helped to transition OZ from a software company to a supplier of Internet-based distribution services. All of the customers and end-users loved the web interface and features of the "Emerald" software.

Tim could see that Dora was on the OZ web page playing with the Emerald product on her laptop. "I've always thought of Emerald and its interface as the gem of OZ," Tim said with a childish grin. "We believe in eating our own dog food here. Everyone uses Emerald for their own operations so that we can make sure the customers are happy. If we have trouble using it, we know it won't be any easier for our customers."

"What a great concept. This is much like what we do at Marvelous, customers always come first, but we eat our own snacks instead of dog food," said Dora with a grin. They both chuckled.

Dora had read the files on Eve's laptop and could see from the organizational health scores that Tim's department was one of the best places to work in OZ. Tim, was a people person; he hired the right managers and encouraged them to hire the right people as well. However, the results from Engineering were not following in the same success pattern they had in the past few years. Projects were getting more and more delayed, customer complaints were on the rise, and although still profitable, the margins and sales had leveled off and were heading down the wrong road.

Just before Tim had arrived for the meeting, Dora had been intently reading an email from Mitchell to Eve describing his thoughts on Tim's department. "Engineering is overstaffed, and they seem to have too much fun there to get any real work done. It is no more than a haven for buddies. We need to axe a bucket-load of the unproductive prima donnas and send a message to the rest of the organization." This raised some concerns for Dora, but she was genuinely interested in hearing Tim's assessment before she drew her own conclusions.

"Tim, as you know, I am here to see if there is any synergy between Marvelous and OZ, so collectively we can figure out if a merger is a win-win for our two companies. I can see people love to work in your well-oiled organization..." Dora said. Pausing for a moment she wanted to say 'but' and then remembered what The Professor had taught her. 'Don't mix messages, remove the *buts* and add the *ands*. Respect the other person by giving them the first chance to explain.' So she continued, "...*and* OZ had some good years."

Tim hesitated for a moment, "You are right about people in my organization, we always seem to have a long line of candidates waiting when we open up new jobs. We've had some great years, *and* the last few haven't met my expectations."

"Bingo," thought Dora, "The Professor was always right."

With a sigh, Tim said, "We all work hard, but as we have grown, departments are working more in silos than as a team. It's not that we don't want to work with one another, just that each one of my peers has specific deliverables and helping us doesn't get them any extra points on their annual performance reviews. Sure Glenda has sent us to some great training classes and workshops. But once we get back into the workplace we're overwhelmed with so many tasks that we get swept up in the day-to-day activity and then we have to hunker down to just stay afloat. Sometimes I guess it becomes hard to see the forest through the trees."

Dora sensed the frustration in his voice and replied, "Tim, it's not unusual for companies to become silo-structured as they grow. What happens naturally when a company is small takes more of a concerted effort after it reaches a certain size. We learned that the hard way at Marvelous. Fortunately we started to pay attention to the leading indicators instead of just the lagging indicators."

"Leading and lagging indicators?" inquired Tim. "I know we track our sales, margins, headcount, and capital expenditures. When they start to go south, we are quick to react and do whatever it takes to make them go in the right direction. Everyone pitches in, we're all involved and we always manage to get through the darkest part of the forest."

"Well you seem to have that piece nailed down. It's the leading indicators like employee engagement, personal empowerment, job satisfaction, and undesirable turnover that give you the clues to what your lagging indicators will be," explained Dora.

"Oh, I see," said Tim as his engineering mind pondered the cause and effect relationship. "But I guess as you have seen from the organizational health scorecard that employees in the Engineering Department are very happy. I personally take a genuine interest in employee development and growth, and on a daily basis I can see that my managers inspire people to create something they really care about."

Dora responded, "Your people are happy, and your turnover is one of the lowest in the company, although Glenda did tell me that you've lost five of the top ten key designers and developers in the last two years?"

"That's right, but it is a very small percent for the number of people we have. Our technical turnover is well below the industry average," Tim said confidently.

"Tim, averages usually mask hidden problems. Would 50% undesirable turnover be a red flag for you?" Dora asked inquisitively.

"Are you kidding? Glenda would have my head on the chopping block," Tim fired back.

"How many of your key designers did you want to keep?" Dora asked cautiously.

"All of them of course!" Tim said vehemently and then paused. She could see the gears turning in Tim's head. "We did lose half of the designers that we wanted to keep, so I suppose my 'undesired' turnover is about 50%. Well that's a different way to look at it, but I get your point."

Tim's whole body language changed as if he had just ripped his own heart out. "I'm not sure what I could have done to create an even better working environment. I was unhappy for weeks after each one of the five key designers left, some even went to our competitors," Tim relented.

"Dora, I love this place and the people that work here. We truly listen to one another, our mantra before each of our meetings is to 'check your titles and egos at the door.' We want all the ideas out on the table whether you are a technician or a PhD." Tim explained.

Dora replied, "Tim, it may not be your department practices that are causing the undesired turnover. How easy is it for your staff to work with the other departments?"

Tim paused, and then he said, "Everyone at OZ is pretty easy-going as long as you don't start messing in their sandbox. We avoid conflict like the plague. Witchell seems to stir up enough conflict with his tirades in our Program Reviews; it's not a pleasant sight. We try to make the rest of the working time more cordial."

"Tirades?" asked Dora.

"I've got stories that would even make Eve-L spin in her grave," Tim said as he rolled his eyes.

"Tell me more," Dora prodded.

Chapter 7 - Marvelous Leadership Secrets

☐ **29.** Do what it takes to keep your best talent.
☐ **30.** Monitor your lagging indicators (financial), but manage by the leading indicators (people).
☐ **31.** Tear down the silos, and instill the virtues of collaboration.
☐ **32.** Provide only purposeful training to achieve sustainable results.

Chapter 8: The Journey's Just Begun

The best strategy for building a competitive organization is to help individuals become more of who they truly are.

— Marcus Buckingham

Tim continued to relate his stories. "Dora, our next sporadic Program Review Meeting is coming up. None of us really look forward to the beatings," Tim said with frustration.

Just then Cher knocked on the door to the conference room and peeked her head in. "Sorry to interrupt, but I think I left my pen and notebook somewhere in here this morning."

"Come in Cher," said Dora.

Cher pushed the door open. "It should only take me a second to find my notebook." She pulled out one of the chairs from the conference table to see her red notebook nestled there.

Tim said to Cher, "I imagine you will need that for the Program Review."

"Exactly Tim, you know how we all love those surprises Witchell drops on us, no matter how well we prepare," Cher said.

Just then, Mitchell's dark backlit figure appeared at the entrance of the open conference room door. "Looks like a party here," Mitchell said with a smirk, as he entered the room. "I expect that you are all working hard on your presentations for the Program Review that is coming up?"

Dora, Tim, and Cher stared at each other for a moment, surprised by Mitchell's arrival.

"We were just talking about that," Cher remarked.

"From my calculations, our projects are burning money faster than we are earning it," Mitchell said sarcastically, "and quite frankly, from a financial perspective, I can't see it helping Ms. Dora here to come up with positive scores for her merger evaluation. I'm off to another one of those damn analyst calls." Leaving more than a hint of negativity behind, Mitchell departed from the room.

"My!" exclaimed Dora, "People come and go so quickly around here."

"Welcome to OZ," said Tim. "People work on internet time and time is money."

"That dreaded Program Review, the end of quarter design deadlines, the performance reviews, and now the merger assessment--all need to be finished. I really don't see how I'm going to get it all done in time," Tim whimpered.

"It's happening all over again, this time each year for the last two years has been the same. We were forced to take on so much firefighting, that it results in poor quality and complete demoralization. As the next quarter begins, we erase the previous turmoil from our memories and restart the madness. It's time we stopped being overly optimistic but it's hard to say no. Our customers have been waiting for the Emerald 2.0 software. Snags in the IT infrastructure are causing us to get further behind in our shipments, staff meetings, design reviews, monthly reports, and of course, the dreaded Program Review." Tim remarked as he swung nervously in his chair.

Cher chimed in, "It's not much different in my land either."

Dora walked over to Tim and lightly touched his shoulders as he was leaning forward on the table. "Tim, it sounds like you are a bit stretched, and you have a lot of this on your own shoulders. How is your staffing, and what do you think it will take to get your head above water?"

"I am at full headcount, of course we could always use more people, but I don't think that's a problem. I just don't know what to do next." Tim said with a frown.

Dora bent over to look at Tim eye to eye. "What does your heart tell you, Tim?"

"Well I am not sure, but what I do know is that I have at least five of my staff, all of whom should be working on Emerald 2.0, who are dealing with fallout from customer problems and unfortunately, with our antiquated IT infrastructure. Sorry Cher!" Tim said somewhat apologetically.

"No offense taken, Tim, I've already whined to Dora about my woes," Cher said, relieved with the Tim's corroboration of the information she had shared with Dora earlier.

Dora sat down next to Tim, "My philosophy has been that no one can be considered successful, unless the team is successful. Sometimes, that letting people help beyond what is within their job description, to help rally for a cause will motivate employees to work even harder. With the Emerald 2.0 delay it sure sounds like the team already knows what the rallying cry would be. Professor Marv always said,

'People don't have to like you, but they need to respect you.' It sounds like your people already like you, so actually making the hard calls, even if it feels harsh, may gain that added level of respect."

Tim looked over at Cher, "Do you think the engineering team respects me?"

"I know they love you as a boss, and with that kind of admiration I can't see their not stepping up to help. I suspect your making more of the hard calls can only add to your respect quotient." Cher said with a smile.

"You always have a way to cut to the bottom line without making me feel worse," Tim chuckled.

Tim leaned over to Cher, and said, "I suppose I could spare some of my engineers, they have already been plugging the holes for the underfunded IT infrastructure you have had to endure. Until you squeeze some budget money out of Witchell's wallet for a new system, maybe they can help patch the foundation software problems and we'll be able to reduce our firefighting. That would finally give us the time back to finish the Emerald 2.0 software. Having convinced himself through his last statement, Tim stood up and announced, "Damn it, let's do it! My heart says it's the right thing to do."

"Great," thought Dora. "It was not about having all the right answers but asking the right questions. Then let the individuals discover the solutions themselves. This way it became their idea and you had instant agreement."

Dora realized she had to ensure Tim's commitment actually happened, and it happened quickly. IT and Engineering were now linked, but from what Dora saw on the sales and marketing files on Eve's laptop, the next meeting with Howard could be a deal breaker.

Chapter 8 - Marvelous Leadership Secrets

☐ **33.** Know when to ask for help.

☐ **34.** Don't confuse activity with accomplishment.

☐ **35.** Ask the right questions and then listen intently.

☐ **36.** Prioritize projects and be willing to de-commit when resources are limited.

☐ **37.** Maintain ownership of the job until it is done or delegated.

THE LEADER OF OZ

Chapter 9: The Lyon's Den

Courage is not simply one of the virtues, but the form of every virtue...at the point of highest reality.

– C.S. Lewis

Howard Lee Lyon was fifty years old, with a stocky body, hippie hair, tomato-red whiskers, and a swollen countenance that nervously held a timid smile. He looked older than his years. There were heavy bags under his eyes and the lines on his face showed signs of anxiety and exhaustion.

Howard's vast technical knowledge of the OZ products had won him the respect of many in the workplace. He knew what customers needed and how to position OZ's products to them. Over his twelve years at OZ, he had earned his promotions by virtue of his technical ability. His loyalty to the company was unquestioned. In his current position, which he assumed less than a year ago, Howard was now responsible for managing all of the marketing and sales team for the company.

Mild and gentle, it was not in him to deny much to his colleagues, who too often took him for granted. Confrontations made him palpitate and stammer. Much to his embarrassment, Howard was aware that his coworkers saw him as a lion with the bite of a pussycat. Despite having a good command of his job, Howard utterly lacked confidence and the ability to take risks.

He had heard the rumor that OZ was in the midst of an evaluation for a merger. "The merger,"

Howard's soul sang with desperate hope, "could be my opportunity to break free from this dreadful position." Howard's heart started beating fast and he hopped out of his seat from apprehension when he received a call from Dora to set up a time to meet with him the next day.

The next day, as was her habit, Dora arrived ten minutes early for the meeting and saw that Howard was having a one-on-one meeting in the conference room with one of his direct reports, Jong Woo. From their body language, Dora could sense that the meeting was not going well. An aggressive-looking Jong appeared to be scolding Howard who sat there listening fearfully. Their meeting ended late, as Jong stormed out of the room in a huff.

Dora found a flustered Howard wiping the sweat off his forehead with his handkerchief. As she ushered herself into the room, Howard tried to compose himself. Rainbo, excited at Howard's furry look, ran toward him, almost toppling him over his chair. Dora cried out, "Stay, Rainbo!" Rainbo froze. She apologized to Howard and offered him a hand as he regained his balance.

"I am really afraid of dogs," lamented Howard.

Dora apologized again, but was surprised that a man as large as Howard should be afraid of such a delicate little animal.

After brief greetings, Howard said, with a blush, "Sorry the meeting with Jong ran over. I told him of our meeting at 11, but he would not stop."

Dora quipped, "Did you have a rough meeting?" Dora had already given Howard an idea about the purpose of the meeting, so he opened up to her quickly.

"We were discussing a customer design for our Emerald 2.0 software, a project that is running behind schedule. We are depending on this project to be successful, as this is expected to be our main revenue generator for next year."

Sympathetically, Dora inquired, "What is delaying the project?"

"Some people have not been delivering on their commitments, so I have had to carry their weight along with mine. I have not slept in weeks from the stress. I try to be sensitive to people's needs, but some are really taking things for granted. For example, Jong claims to be having problems with his motorcycle for several weeks. He's been coming in late and leaving early. He did not like it, to put it mildly, when I explained the situation and told him that he should have the courtesy to keep me and his other teammates informed of his inability to deliver on his commitments."

Looking at Howard with great wonder, Dora said, "As a manager you have the responsibility to hold people accountable for their actions or inactions."

Clawing his fluorescent beard, Howard responded with dejection, "I suppose I am not very good at that. Even in my previous jobs, I have always been afraid of facing people. Based on my position, I could somehow have people do what they needed to do. But if they ever tried to confront me, I ended up backing down. I just cannot handle conflict."

Surprised at his desperate honesty and openness, Dora said, "This does not seem right. The others on Glenda's staff tell me you are a good person, and you are great at your job. You should not be hindered because of your weakness in certain skills that can be learned."

Changing gears smoothly, Dora continued, "I am going to need your help over the next two weeks as we evaluate the viability of the merger between OZ and Marvelous."

"But I am already running late on my project. I can hardly risk digressing into other activities," Howard said with some disdain.

Dora returned, "How about we cut a deal? You help me with my evaluation, and I will help you get your project back on track." Howard had heard of Dora's accomplishments from his fellow teammates, Cher and Tim, and was very eager to hear what she had to say. Suddenly, he felt a glimmer of hope. He knew that this was perhaps his only opportunity to get his insufferable work-life balanced and back in order. With a leap of faith, he agreed to Dora's giving offer.

Dora said, "We're better off when we face our fears and grow from those experiences. I'm learning a lot through this journey and I'll be happy to have you as a partner and friend."

Rainbo nudged closer and closer to Howard as the conversation progressed. Howard appeared to be getting more at ease with the small creature. A new friendship between the two was just beginning.

The brief comforting silence was shattered when the phone in the conference room started ringing. Dora answered it on speakerphone and heard Mitchell's voice abruptly bellowing out "I'm looking for Howard. Is he there with you?"

Howard had always been secretly scared of Mitchell and had kept his distance from him whenever possible. He would interact with Mitchell only when necessary, such as at Glenda's staff meeting. Howard spoke in a nervous tone "Y...yes, I'm here, Mitchell."

"I want you to be ready for the Program Review this week," demanded the voice.

"Mitchell, I thought it was not due until the beginning of next quarter," sought Howard meekly with his breath falling short. "I want them earlier this time, so get to it now," boomed Mitchell, and with a click, the phone went dead.

As Howard trembled slightly, Dora knew that Mitchell was throwing yet another monkey wrench in the works to slow her down.

Chapter 9 - Marvelous Leadership Secrets

☐ **38.** Integrate the uniqueness of each person into the organization.

☐ **39.** Understand that followers are the reason leaders exist.

☐ **40.** Use good management practices to go beyond the status-quo.

☐ **41.** Develop the proficiency to deal with conflict and change.

☐ **42.** Be prepared to sacrifice your likability to maintain or gain respect.

Chapter 10: Being a Lyon in the Face of Fear

*Whether you think you can or whether you think
you can't, you're right.*

– Henry Ford

The silence in the room was palpable. Howard sat there, his face curled up like an enormous rotund prune, looking like a juggler who had been handed far too many sharp knives. Dora laid a cool hand on his trembling one, and referring to what had transpired with Mitchell, she said, "This isn't right, and you must face this situation with courage."

"I know," retorted Howard. "What would you do in my place?"

Dora's thoughts flashed back to Professor Marv who had always demonstrated to her that confidence develops from taking deliberate steps in the face of challenges, obstacles and imperfect conditions. In Howard, she had discovered some critical attributes of a leader such as his cognitive skills. All he really lacked was a little self-confidence. He only needed a nudge to start to take incremental risks, learn from mistake, and accept success. She knew that small successes would bring him a clearer sense of his values and talents, and enable him to deal more maturely with complex situations and people.

As the manager of Human Resources at Marvelous Snacks, Dora had extensively used a face-the-fear technique to get people out of their shells. She would ask people to engage in the very activity they were afraid of, such as public speaking, and help them prevent the response caused by their fear, such as running away or backing down. Having them stay with the fear and overcoming it through practice ultimately assisted them in becoming less affected by their fear. Dora likened Howard to the eagle, which having been brought up in the company of chickens, started believing that he was a chicken until he was nudged to fly. The majestic flight made him gain back his true self-identify and confidence.

"If I were in your place," Dora replied, "I would first start with the project, which seems to be stretching you too thin for lack of support on the part of some team members. At Marvelous, we implemented breakthrough systems to ensure that the highest possible, clearly defined goals were set for each member of the team. Every member had full control of his or her resources, and clear measurements were in place to help everyone easily track their own progress. If you do this and deal with people honestly and rewarding them for their successes while also holding them accountable, you will find that your group will start acting like a team." As Howard watched with lit-up eyes, Dora showed him some examples of the project processes on her laptop. She demonstrated how Zach, Hank, and Hillary had implemented this method at Marvelous Snacks to achieve a breakthrough for specific projects in their respective organizations.

"I was fortunate to have a coach and mentor like Professor Marv who taught me through role modeling that confidence is contagious. Only a confident leader can instill confidence in his or her followers. It is easier to inspire employees to take on challenging tasks and achieve success when you visibly exhibit self-confidence yourself. It doesn't mean you are arrogant or a know-it-all, you can be humble and strong willed, and still be sure about yourself. Confidence, just like any other skill, can be learned through practice. Once you believe in yourself, others will too.

"You have to be willing to step forward, enjoy competition, be eager to work with others, and have the desire to achieve success for yourself, for your employees *and* for your organization. Therefore, this is the second aspect that I would focus on developing. There are specific self-assessments and activities that can help you get on track. If you would like, we can work together to help you grow in this area."

Howard's heart pounded in delight that someone like Dora seemed genuinely interested in helping him take positive strides to grow. His joy however was short-lived as his thoughts faded back to what the wretched Mitchell had requested just minutes before. There was a lot of real work that had to be done, so he began questioning in his mind whether Dora's promise was just an unrealistic dream, as much as his heart wanted it to be true.

Sensing Howard's dilemma, Dora added, "This may be the time for your first face-your-fear session with Mitchell. I would suggest that you have a sit-down with him to negotiate the review that he has requested from you relative to your project priorities. Remember that you can remain humble even as you are strong and confident.

"Howard, the collective futures of our companies are at stake. I would like to have you with me on my journey over the next few weeks as we do an honest evaluation for the merger. If we can face the short-term challenges, the future will be bright for people on both sides. I would like to know if I can count on your partnership and help."

Howard's blood rushed to his face in anxiety, but he saw clearly that the need to correct his course was now. He had to act for himself *and* for others whose futures depended on OZ.

He retorted to Dora, "I am with you, but I want you to do one favor just for me." After a long pause, he added, "Talk me out of it!" with a nervous, semi-confident smile.

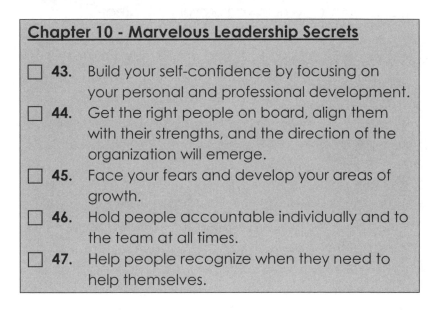

Chapter 10 - Marvelous Leadership Secrets

☐ **43.** Build your self-confidence by focusing on your personal and professional development.

☐ **44.** Get the right people on board, align them with their strengths, and the direction of the organization will emerge.

☐ **45.** Face your fears and develop your areas of growth.

☐ **46.** Hold people accountable individually and to the team at all times.

☐ **47.** Help people recognize when they need to help themselves.

Chapter 11: Getting the Monkeys Off Our Backs

Knowledge has to be improved, challenged, and increased constantly, or it vanishes.
– Peter F. Drucker

Dora sat down in front of her laptop collecting her thoughts for the group meeting with Cher, Tim, and Howard that was scheduled to start in 30 minutes. A tone from her computer announced the arrival of a new email from Professor Marv's assistant, Emma Martinez.

"Rainbo, let's hope for some good news," Dora said softly.

The email was short and to the point, characteristic of Emma. It read, "The Professor's color has returned, but the tests are still inconclusive. He is still under observation in the ICU and doctors are cautiously optimistic. I will keep you posted." This small bit of news helped put Dora's mind at ease.

With a momentary sense of peace, she sat back in her chair and regained composure, quickly typing to capture her thoughts for the next meeting.

"Cher knows the ins and outs of IT, loves the numbers, and given enough time to collect her thoughts, comes up with data-driven solutions. She wants to help, but becomes scattered when she tries to make decisions.

"Tim, on the other hand, can't be bothered with numbers. He cares deeply about people, but lacks the heart or the ability to express his care through actions. People trust Tim and love to be in his company. He is quick to act but when the company has big projects to complete, he is not their first choice.

"And then there is Howard. He is the ultimate team member, but is quite emotional. Each of the three has recognized that the current environment is insufferable."

As Dora rehearsed for her next few encounters with the trio, she experienced a fleeting moment of doubt. She quickly dismissed her reservations as she recalled Professor Marv's words, "If you don't have concerns as you enter the land of change, you are not pushing the edge of possibilities."

The trio arrived at the doorway of the conference room. After some brief small talk, Dora asked, "Would you like to know about a people alignment process that we've successfully used for years at Marvelous Snacks? Everything begins with having the right people in the right seats. We managers typically define 'right' as matching skills to tasks. When we did this, we found that the work was getting done. However, we discovered that our employees were becoming more and more disengaged. The flow of creativity was slowing and new ideas were drying up." Cher, Tim, and Howard listened intently.

Dora continued, "About seven years ago, one of our consultants introduced us to a simple process. This process identifies a person's ideal mixture of the three types of tasks that we all do as part of our personal and professional lives — routine, troubleshooting, and project. Routine tasks are the ones that are predictable and need to be done immediately or in a short amount of time."

Howard quickly interrupted, "Kind of like what I do the first thing every morning when I distribute new inquiry emails to the appropriate sales people?"

"Exactly! The second is troubleshooting or problem-solving tasks. These tasks are unpredictable but also need to be done immediately."

Cher chimed in, "Would our server fire this morning be one of those?"

"Bingo," said Dora, "and the third type are the project tasks, which *are* predictable but don't need to get done immediately."

Tim spoke up, "Welcome to my world. We've got so many design projects in the pipeline that I can hardly keep track of all the activity."

Dora leaned back with a smile, "You guys get it! Now all we have to do is figure out what your own mixtures are, and we'll be ready for the second part of the process." Each of them looked a bit confused.

As she wrote a web site address on the conference room whiteboard, Dora said, "Open up your laptops and go to this web site and take a quick five-minute online assessment. Once you've done that, I'll have your task preferences, and then we can quickly move to Part Two." The trio logged in and eagerly began answering the short 15 question survey. It was almost as if they were kids opening birthday presents. Instantly, their assessment results arrived in Dora's inbox.

"Give me a minute and I'll grab your results from the printer." Dora walked down the hall to the printer, which was spitting out their reports. As she picked up each of the diverse profile results, she immediately could see that the next step in the process would be an interesting one. Dora reentered the conference room and handed them their 'presents.'

"Take a few minutes to read your reports and then we'll begin the fun part."

Cher, Tim, and Howard poured over the results with smiles and astonishment. "This is me to a tee," said Tim, and the others nodded in agreement.

"The pie charts you have in your reports show the ideal mixture of how you'd like to spend 100% of your time split between the three types of tasks. Getting your actual job to look like your ideal job is how you will become the most satisfied, empowered, and engaged employees. It is here that your intrinsic motivation, the stuff inside that gives you that continuous rush of adrenaline, is maximized. I quickly looked at your reports and you'll note that each of your charts looks different."

"Which mixture is the best?" asked Cher impatiently.

"There isn't a best one, but there is an optimized one for every job," Dora said as she began moving back to the whiteboard, picking up a marker to make some notes for the group to see.

"Tim, you like lots of Project work. You are OK with some problem solving, but routine work is very low on your priority list."

"Yup, pretty much sums up my job. I love the project work, but I still have too much problem solving and routine work to do," Tim said self-assuredly.

"Howard," said Dora "your chart looks almost the opposite of Tim's. You don't like the projects and would prefer more routine and problem-solving work."

Howard thought for a moment, "Sales and marketing, that's my kind of job. Give me a customer problem and enough time and I'll trap it like a mouse."

All the others laughed, Howard was a character and he usually had some unique anecdotes to give others a visual of what he was describing. "I don't like the tedious detail and planning in the project work, but I realize sometimes you just have to do that stuff," Howard concluded.

Cher, still analyzing her report, asked in a somewhat concerned tone, "And mine? All of my task preference percentages are about the same. So what does that tell you about me? I can't make up my mind? I don't have any strong preferences one way or another?"

"Quite the contrary, Cher," Dora quickly responded. "Your report indicates that you have more flexibility doing any of the three task types. You like balance, and dealing with lots of variety keeps your batteries charged."

Cher sat up in her chair. "Yes, I do love the variety; the more multi-tasking the better. I guess that is me and with your description, it actually sounds like a good thing," Cher said confidently.

Dora continued, "I am really glad to see that all of you understand the concept. Now, let's go on to the second step. Remember I had asked you this morning to do a quick summary of your regular tasks? Now let's segment them into one of the three task types and we'll see how your jobs match up with your ideal mixture."

As they each categorized their tasks, Dora could see some growing concern that their ideal and actual mixtures were not aligned.

"OK, now what? None of our actual mixtures look like our ideal mixtures. Guess we'll all have to quit and look for other jobs," Cher said jokingly. The others looked equally puzzled.

"Stay with me for just a bit longer. Howard, I see you'd like more routine tasks and less project work. Tim, you have too much problem solving and not enough project work. Cher, you're flexible on all three task types, but you would like more of a challenge with some problem solving and a reduction in your routine work. Can you see any patterns here?" Dora asked, aiming to draw them in.

They all sat there for a moment trying to absorb what Dora had just revealed.

Tim said, "I think it's pretty simple. It looks like each of us is doing too much of what we like least and not enough of what we like most. Maybe the three of us could swap tasks so we're doing more of what motivates us? Is that the hidden message here, Dora?"

Dora felt like she had created a breakthrough. "Tim, you know sometimes you don't give yourself enough credit for how smart you really are," she said, patting Tim on his back.

"Now it really is up to you. At Marvelous Snacks, we normally do this process with the manager in the room, but with Glenda's schedule, you'll have to empower yourselves to create the solutions and then take them to Glenda for approval instead of working through the answers with her," Dora said with a confident smile.

Cher rolled her chair back and said in excitement, "Imagine how much fun it would be to start working across our functions... and all the learning that would happen!"

Howard added, "Isn't this a great growth opportunity for all of us? I'd love to get back to my roots doing a bit more technical design work. I've got more project work than what my ideal task balance needs. Let's reinvent our jobs."

Tim said, "If we can do this at our level, it looks like we can get more work done, and actually have more fun doing it! Is that the message, and if so, shouldn't we be doing this for our staffs too?"

Dora smiled. "Yes, you'll discover what we've been experiencing for the last seven years at Marvelous Snacks: you leave your job at the end of the day feeling incredibly productive, engaged, empowered, motivated, and fulfilled. It makes coming back the next day that much more exciting. And yes, you should be doing this for your staff. It opens up great opportunities for creativity, but one step at a time. If you can demonstrate that it works for you, leading by example, your staff will accept it wholeheartedly."

With that final statement, the three of them nodded in agreement and busily started the exercise of swapping tasks. A short time after completing the process, Dora noticed a small piece of paper with one task on it, that each of them had pushed away like it was poison. A task seemed to be looming over all of them.

Dora said, "I see that there is this one task that each of you has excluded from your new ideal mixture of tasks. Let's put that one aside for a few minutes. I am betting we'll see it reemerge at the conclusion of the next process." Cher, Tim and Howard all looked curious but also somewhat relieved.

Chapter 11 - Marvelous Leadership Secrets

☐ **48.** Gain an understanding of what motivates you and your employees.

☐ **49.** Encourage your employees to create solutions.

☐ **50.** Align people's jobs to their ideal balance of tasks.

☐ **51.** Allow flexibility across functions for improved learning and results.

☐ **52.** Trust the passions of your workers to bring strength to their jobs.

Chapter 12: Developing a Sense of Purpose

People do not care about how much you know until they know how much you care.
— John Maxwell

A deep-seated team spirit was beginning to develop among the 'Gang of Four' as they worked together with support, trust, affection, and acceptance of one another. Dora's job alignment exercise had given Cher, Tim and Howard visibility about how they could optimize their jobs. The three realized the importance of job alignment more than ever and now were eager to ensure that their own employees also fit well in their jobs, which was the key to effectiveness, engagement, and fulfillment.

Dora's purpose was to help Cher, Tim and Howard to find freedom from the prison of their own supposed limitations so they could be more fulfilled at work and in life. She had their best interest at heart, coaching them with care and sincerity. Indeed, her three protégés were learning and growing, seeing new possibilities, and gaining confidence, ready to experience new challenges. She was their ally. She was their catalyst. She was their supporter. She was their mentor!

Over the past few days, Dora had discovered something else that was very refreshing from observing them. They had slowly opened up to each other and to her about their fears, challenges and vulnerabilities. In her moments of indecision, Cher would turn to Tim and Howard, each of whom would encourage and affirm her through the decision-making process until she herself marveled at how clearly she seemed to know what to do.

With Tim, what his heart desired would be supported by Cher and Howard. In one instance, when Tim was feeling down from thinking about a hospitalized employee in his group, Cher and Howard prodded him to call and inquire about the employee's health and lend his support. The glow on Tim's face after the call, from having walked down his heart's path, was an accolade enough for Howard and Cher.

Howard, who would normally run from confrontations, oddly began demonstrating an interest, and what's more, less exasperation and worry, about team activities. Tim and Cher's dedication had much to do with this transformation in Howard. Dora noted that the three friends had turned into peer-coaches for one another.

Strangely, in the middle of the team's progress and Dora's feelings of happiness, a tinge of sadness suddenly hit her as she remembered Professor Marv and his poor health. She wondered how he was doing and her heart became heavy as she remembered the doctor's inconclusive prognosis. She so badly wanted to pick up the phone and talk to him, but she didn't. The task ahead of her was absolutely critical to the health of Marvelous Snacks, which she considered her family. She could not afford to let down the people in Kansas who were depending on her. She had to help Professor Marv uncover a new direction for their company just as wonderful as the path they had traveled so far, if not better. Being fully aware of Dora's stresses and strains, Cher, Tim and Howard often made jokes to keep her amused and cheerful.

Wanting to gain a deeper understanding of the alignment between the people and the processes at OZ, Dora began, "Now that we have a good understanding of how we can narrow the gap between actual and optimized jobs, let's talk about the planning process at OZ. How are projects selected?"

Cher replied, "Very simple. It is all about the return-on-investment. Witchell goes straight to the bottom line at the planning meeting. His sole criterion for project selection is money. As we always say, 'If it is doesn't render money, it's not Witchell's honey!'"

Tim added, "Cher's right. He doesn't care whether the project aligns with people or organizational structure. Witchell would have the poor engineers and computer scientists dig up the entire OZ campus with their own bare hands if he received a tip that there was gold buried under this building."

Not to be left out of the banter, Howard added, "And Eve-L's heart was as dark as the color of her sunglasses. If one of us protested to what she and Witchell wanted, she would promptly get back at us, as surely as the lion is the king of the jungle, with some type of covert punishment, be it endless, unnecessary work with artificial priorities, budget cuts, or denial of training requests. We learned that risk-taking was not safe in meetings with those two and we had to think twice before speaking our minds."

Dora recalled some emails she had reviewed on Eve's laptop. One of them was an exchange between Eve and Mitchell joking triumphantly about how they had forced Cher, Tim and Howard to comply with a particular course of action. Disturbed about the extent of the disconnection within the organization, Dora inquired, "What about Glenda? Doesn't she help in the mediation of the differences and disconnects?"

Tim returned, "Glenda is a great person and used to be closely involved in organizational matters. When she was available, OZ was doing great and we were the envy of the industry. However, over the past two years, she has been extremely occupied outside of the company, leaving the business to run on auto-pilot."

Cher added, "We have written to her about some of our missteps and about the covert conduct of Eve-L and Witchell. However, without hard evidence, it is so difficult to tie them down without sounding like whiners. We have not seen any response from Glenda as of yet."

Howard said, "Well, it is possible that she is investigating the matter thoroughly before getting back to us? It is also possible that she got interested in this merger *because* she wanted to do a little house cleaning here at OZ?"

Pushing her suspicions about Eve and Mitchell's misdeeds to the background of her mind, Dora decided to help the trio continue their momentum on absorbing change without losing focus. So she said, "Well, if you would like, I could give you an overview of the planning process we use at Marvelous Snacks. Perhaps it will give you some ideas on project selection and priority setting." They were eager to hear her best practices.

Dora continued, "Our approach evaluates projects from five perspectives: employees, customers, stakeholders, finance, and learning and development. We create a map on which we tabulate the points on these five aspects for each of the projects on the table. Our goal is to ensure that every project we select maximizes the strengths of our employees, serves our customers and stakeholders in the best possible way, produces the best financial returns, and allows for continuous growth and development of our organization. We have found that the synthesis of these perspectives yields the best project decisions and sustained results." Dora then took the three keen learners through specific examples utilizing her laptop.

After answering their questions and ensuring that they had fully grasped the concept, Dora inquired, "Are you ready to try this for your organizations?"

Tim was the first to speak, "I'm really excited and cannot wait try this new approach!"

"Great. Let's spend the next hour planning and prioritizing the immediate tasks you have on hand."

For an energetic hour, the hustle and bustle of drafting plans and tables on flipcharts, whiteboards, and laptops continued. Dora remained a comfortable distance from the team letting them each work independently to gain confidence with the process while remaining available to answer their questions. Finally, Cher, Tim, and Howard were ready to share their findings with one another.

Dora was impressed to find nice maps of projects with all of the process steps completed. It appeared that each of them had developed a good sense of how their projects and tasks could be rearranged to achieve the best possible overall outcome. Not surprisingly, the same task they had pushed outside of their ideal task mixtures in the previous hour's exercise fell to the bottom of each of their priority lists... the Program Review! Since they had worked independently on their lists, they were a bit surprised to find this as a common element.

All turning toward Dora, Cher was the first to speak this time, "We think the Program Reviews are good and definitely have value; however, they must not distract from the primary activities that add value to the company. Since we just had a Program Review two weeks ago, we don't believe having one again this week makes any sense. It would be good to have the next review in another month's time consistent with our normal frequency of Project milestones."

In her mind, Dora suspected that Mitchell had thrown in the Program Review artificially to keep these managers busy and unavailable to help her with the merger evaluations, but she did not express this suspicion to her three friends. Letting them make their own decisions, Dora inquired, "What would you like to do?"

Cher responded, "I think we should communicate our concerns to Mitchell."

Tim added, "That would be the right thing to do."

And Howard returned, "Yes, it's time to stand up and speak out." With that, all three arose and headed down the long hallway toward Mitchell's office.

Mitchell was sitting with Wingo on his shoulder. "Can we have a word with you?" His huge head turned as a red ball of fire when he saw Dora, Cher, Tim, and Howard together.

"What's this all about?" he shot back curtly.

"We've done some analysis on the priorities of our projects and tasks. Glenda always tells us to do the right things in the right way, so we wanted to discuss with you the need to push out our Program Review," Howard spoke, his heart secretly pounding heavily inside.

Mitchell almost exploded. Wingo, looking as angry as his owner, jumped off his shoulder onto the desk as if unable to stand the heat radiating from Mitchell's face.

Mitchell turned to Dora and said, "You have been corrupting our people. You are trying to turn lambs into lions. I take this as a direct attack. You will pay for this! And the three of you, meet me in two hours in my conference room."

With that, Mitchell turned around to face the large window of his corner office, as if he were dismissing the group. A worried-looking Wingo jumped on top of the cubicle wall expecting an attack from his master.

Chapter 12 - Marvelous Leadership Secrets

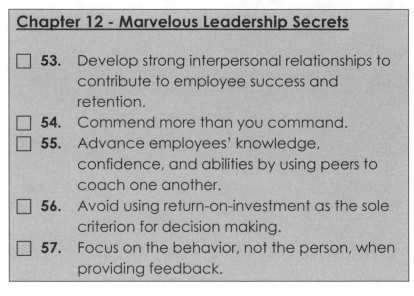

☐ **53.** Develop strong interpersonal relationships to contribute to employee success and retention.

☐ **54.** Commend more than you command.

☐ **55.** Advance employees' knowledge, confidence, and abilities by using peers to coach one another.

☐ **56.** Avoid using return-on-investment as the sole criterion for decision making.

☐ **57.** Focus on the behavior, not the person, when providing feedback.

Chapter 13: Opening the Gates of the City

The leader of the future will be a person who can lead and follow, be central and marginal, be hierarchically above and below, be individualistic and a team player, and above all, be a perpetual learner.

– Edgar H. Schein

They walked out of Mitchell's office with mixed emotions. On the one hand, they were relieved that potentially they could get the Program Review off their plate, but on the other hand, the encounter with Mitchell made them fear that the retribution would be worse than the relief.

"I could really use a walk outside to get some air to clear my brain," Cher said. The rest of them agreed as they got on the elevator heading to the ground floor.

Dora knew they all felt uneasy about the interaction with Mitchell, but working with these three members of Glenda's staff, she felt there was something deeper driving their behaviors.

All OZ employees had the company's values as the background image on their laptops, and Dora had seen the values listed on posters throughout the halls and hanging in other prominent places throughout the building. These people were all proud to be part of OZ, and she could see that they cared about the success of their projects and also for the company itself. The values were simple, 1) *Integrity*–serve by doing what you say, 2) *Innovation*–go beyond your current knowledge, 3) *Results*–deliver to

81

the highest standards, and 4) *Growth*–strive to grow personally, professionally, and financially.

Dora had spent the last week with Cher, Tim and Howard and felt that she knew each of them lived those values. Yet, there still seemed to be something out of place, not all of the puzzle pieces were fitting together. Their interactions continued to improve as she assisted them in helping each other. She sensed there were some unwritten rules that had yet to be put out on the table, which would help her better understand this company's culture.

Dora sat down with them at one of the courtyard tables away from the heavy traffic of the cafeteria area. No one spoke for a while and she could sense that all of them were mentally replaying the events from that morning.

Dora thought of initiating a "Dialog and Appreciative Inquiry" session that she had used extensively at Marvelous Snacks. "Would you be interested in a short, fun activity to help us test the OZ values of *Innovation* and *Growth*?" Dora asked.

"Anything that can help clear my mind," said Cher. All the others nodded. So Dora began.

"First, I'm going to ask each of you to answer a question. The more honest you are at answering them, the better. The others will not express agreement or disagreement, only just listen intently. Once we are done, we'll have some new insights on what we're getting ready to tackle over the next several days. This process will contribute to the fourth OZ value of *Growth*."

Tim said, "We're game. Let's get started."

"Here's the question: What do you really value about working here?" Dora asked confidently as she turned to Howard. He had a stunned look on his weathered face and sat there for almost a minute stroking his beard as he thought. Dora gave him the time to think and she gestured to Cher and Tim to hold off their urge to disturb the silence.

Howard always took his time and was deliberate about his answers. Dora expected that he would talk about the team and being a part of something bigger. However, what was about to come out of Howard's mouth startled her as well as Tim and Cher.

"I have never thought deeply about that before, Dora. I am guessing you expect me to say something about the great people, how I love my job, or the challenging projects. Those are important, but not what I value most about this place. I love to learn! I'd come in every day even without a paycheck, but please don't tell Glenda that. My kids still need to eat." The others chuckled. "The new knowledge I gain each day is more valuable to me than a pocketful of rubies."

Dora turned to Cher, "How about for you?"

Cher collected her thoughts and said, "I thought I had my response, but listening to Howard is making me rethink my gut reaction. I've always felt that getting a degree was important. I value learning, but it's not a priority for me. The money is important to me. I actually thought that money was important to everyone."

Howard shrugged his shoulders.

Cher continued, "I work here because work is a part of my balance, I value creating meaning for my life and a worthy cause. At the age of six I was diagnosed with an inoperable brain tumor. The doctors told my parents that I probably wouldn't live past my 12th birthday. You can imagine how that would affect your childhood. I prayed every night and never gave up hope. For my 12th birthday, my parents took me on a trip to Australia. I thought this was my last birthday on earth and my parents were making it extra special. It was extra special because that is where I met Dr. Beatrice Frank. She had developed an experimental procedure to remove tumors that were once believed to be inoperable. Money is important to me, but I give a large chunk of my salary to Dr. Frank's clinic. She's 75 years old now and still developing lifesaving procedures."

Dora, Tim, and Howard all sat stunned as Cher concluded her story. They felt inspired by Cher's openness and resilience.

After a long silence, Tim said, "I value two things. First, enjoying what I do while I get lots of work done and second, the rush I get from creative risk taking." Pulling a small index card out of his pocket he said, "I have my own scorecard that I use to secretly hold myself accountable to do the best I can every day that I walk through the front doors of this emerald-striped building. I only put a checkmark on the scorecard if it is a mutual win, meaning that it was accomplished *without* doing it at someone else's expense."

Tim continued, "The second thing I value is the ability to take risks. I had a bad experience in my last company. They publicly encouraged risk taking, it was even one of their values, so I stepped out of my comfort zone for one of the CEO's pet projects. I was the only one willing to take on the challenge and I believed in the project as much as the CEO. Even though we finished the project on time and met all of the CEO's expectations, the results came up short of the customer's needs. Instead of being recognized for all of the 70-hour weeks and role modeling the risk taking value, I arrived one Friday morning and found my office neatly packed for me in four cardboard boxes.

"I know that sometimes I am too conservative here at OZ. I used to like rocking the boat, but carrying those boxes out to my car that day left a lasting impression. I haven't shared that story with anyone outside of my family," Tim concluded with a sigh.

Dora was pleased with the candidness as each of the three shared what they truly valued about working at OZ. She had learned from Professor Marv to hold these dialog sessions with the employees at Marvelous Snacks when they were least expected. Although it felt like a distraction from day-to-day tactical activities, no one ever came away disappointed. It was a small investment in time for these short activities, which helped reinforce the cohesiveness of the team for the hard times.

Chapter 13 - Marvelous Leadership Secrets

☐ **58.** Provide the opportunity to share individual experiences.

☐ **59.** Use dialog to allow listening go beyond just hearing the words.

☐ **60.** Realize that people's values shape their behaviors.

☐ **61.** Know when to take a pause from your daily tasks to help accelerate progress.

Chapter 14: Meeting with The Wizard

The key is not to prioritize what's on your schedule, but to schedule your priorities.
- Stephen R. Covey

Even Rainbo now seemed to be fully engaged as they journeyed across the two worlds. Every step along the way, his eyes, mood and bark reflected the joy, triumph and strains experienced by Dora. It appeared that he could even sense Howard's moments of fear, Cher's indecision, and Tim's unexpressed emotions. If there were a cognition test for dogs, Rainbo would have passed it with flying colors.

That glorious afternoon, his eyes were flashing the joys of the esprit de corps between Dora and the threesome gang as they enjoyed their lunch together.

Then they all received text messages simultaneously from Glenda that read: "Teleconference with Main Investor at four o'clock. Attendance required. I'll be calling in from my home office." Glenda was not the type to send such messages lightly. Sensing how critical the meeting must be, the group packed up and headed to the conference room to review their latest data and refresh their main messages. Dora saw her three friends preparing for the meeting with enthusiasm, passion and confidence.

As they entered the conference room, Mitchell was there chewing on a cigar with his feet sprawled up atop the center table. Wingo sat high-strung by the speakerphone as if anxious for the call. Mitchell neither acknowledged their arrival nor made any effort to accommodate them as they found their seats. The uneasy silence in the room was broken as the phone rang, making Wingo jump several feet in the air.

Mitchell took control of the phone and answered in an upbeat voice, "Mitchell speaking. May I help you?" Wingo's face acquired a puzzled look at his owner's apparent change of attitude. Cher, Tim, Howard, and Dora were fully aware that Mitchell was someone who was always on his best behavior when he was with upper management, but showed a different side when dealing with his peers and those lower in the organizational hierarchy.

"Mitchell, this is Glenda," returned the voice on the phone. "Are Dora, Cher, Tim, and Howard there?"

Dora responded, "Hi Glenda. Yes, we are here."

Glenda continued, "Dora, Mr. Wizir Humbug will be calling in momentarily, so let me take this time to debrief you on the situation. We all warmly call him The Wizard. He holds the majority financial stake in OZ and appears unconvinced about our proposed merger based on his initial reviews. He attributes his doubts to some information he has apparently received from unnamed sources. OZ will be in a crisis if he pulls the funding. He called me with some specific questions, so I thought I would let him get the answers directly from the horses' mouths. I ask you to be open, honest and direct with him."

Dora gulped with nervousness at the thought of the merger falling through, but she quickly pulled herself together.

After a few short clicks, a loud baritone voice announced, *"This is Wizir. Who's on the line?"* Rainbo gazed at the phone with wonder and apprehension. Wingo took refuge under the table, away from his master's feet.

"Hello, Wizir! This is Glenda, and we have my entire staff here—Mitchell, Cher, Tim, and Howard. We also have Dora Gayle from Marvelous Snacks in the room."

Wizir began, *"As we have discussed, Glenda, I am evaluating the data about the merger, which is conflicting at best. I want more inputs and ideas before I make my decision."*

Glenda returned, "I will let each of my staff and Dora speak. They are the closest to the facts. Mitchell, would you like to go first?"

Like a chameleon, Mitchell transformed his tone and began, "I am proud of the policies implemented by my Finance and Human Resources departments, which have ensured that OZ runs like an efficient machine. We are able to design, measure, and manage our processes, products, and people perfectly. We have kept labor costs low, employees come in on time, productivity is on track, spending is under control and our constant restructuring keeps us responsive. These policies have worked well for us in the past and I am sure they will continue to work well in the future. The bottom line is that OZ's success depends on sustaining these efforts. Merging with incompatible types of businesses will leave us terribly uncompetitive in the 21st century." Mitchell's face bore a creepy smile and a façade of Machiavellian duplicity as he glanced mockingly at the other four members in the room. He was convinced that he had successfully fueled more doubts in The Wizard about the merger.

There was a brief uncomfortable silence in the room, and Glenda intervened, "OK. What is your view, Tim?"

Tim responded, "I agree with Mitchell on his point about efficiency, which is allowing us to stay afloat. However, we are facing a growth and sustainability challenge. Our people are burning out, because there is little sense of a shared humanitarian mission in the organization. We may remain viable for the foreseeable future, but at the cost of high employee turnover and unengaged employees. I believe some of Marvelous Snack's philosophies and methods will inject a sense of human inspiration and achievement into our company."

It was Cher's turn to provide her inputs. She began, "We live in the knowledge society, where people are a company's main value proposition. Unfortunately, OZ and our current systems are struggling to keep up with the times. Unless we change the way we think about our people, we will fall. The command-and-control type of culture we have in place is not suitable for sound decision-making and innovation. The lack of empowerment and collaboration in making decisions saps all the energy and focus from employees. In a changing environment, when we ought to be learning and acting faster than our competitors, our current culture is handcuffing us. Without radical rethinking of our modus operandi, I know that our road will run out in due course."

A nervous Howard braced himself up with a short plea under his breath. He knew that this was his chance to speak up for himself, for his people, and for what he truly believed to be the right thing for OZ. So he roared, "The business operations are being conducted without major problems. Sales are on track because employees execute their contract with the company by performing their jobs, as they are required to. However, our employees are not happy. They are angry, anxious and frustrated. We need to have leadership that creates confidence in people who are frightened, instills courage where there is hesitancy, and brings a sense of assurance that our future will be better. This merger is our only opportunity to infuse new leadership and ideas to help in the long run."

After Howard had ended, Glenda came back, "Well, those were all candid and heartfelt inputs. Dora, you have been evaluating our company from an outsider's view. It would be particularly useful to get your honest perspectives." The Wizard remained quiet, but his presence on the call was very palpable.

Drawing on her integrity and personal courage, Dora responded, "My boss, Professor Marv, says that we are facing a true tipping point in the world and particularly in our business. This inflection is being driven by scientific progress, information technology revolution, and cross cultural openness. The question is, are we going to allow this potential to turn into reality? I am convinced that the synergy between the Marvelous Snack's product line and OZ's distribution technology would do wonders for our collective future as we move from a state of unadorned national success to a place of true significance in the world over the next decades.

"I have learned many new things about management and organizations these past few weeks. In Kansas, we practiced leading from the grass roots, where we enable people to organize themselves to realize their maximum potential. This allows leadership to flourish at all levels in the company.

"However, my sense is the most valuable assets at OZ, its people, are being held back through organizational policies that make them afraid to share their ideas. This creates a huge perceived distance of power among ranks, promotes unhealthy group behaviors, and reduces risk taking. There is little to no action taken on employee feedback, which breeds resentment, frustration, and is demoralizing. Human Resources cannot be treated like Finance or Accounting. People should be treated like humans, not like machines, numbers or rules. There are neither simple causes nor magic fixes to these issues, nor is there one 'bad' person to blame. The potential for greatness exists here at OZ, but these issues will need to be addressed to liberate this latent power."

Mitchell's face became fiery red and he looked ready to disgorge flames out of his mouth, but before he could utter a word, The Wizard thundered in, *"My information does not match your claims. However, you are implying some crucial roadblocks in the status quo, so I want to give you one more chance to bring me concrete evidence by next Thursday. If you fail to do so, this merger deal is dead. Glenda, call me immediately on my cell phone. This meeting is over."*

With that, the meeting came to an abrupt end, as the dial tone signaled that The Wizard and Glenda had left the conference call.

Feeling encouraged by The Wizard's demands on Dora, Mitchell confidently stood, his eyebrows cocked up all the way to the top of his forehead, and left the room with a look of triumph on his face. Wingo stuck out his tongue at the group inside as the conference room door closed on his face.

"I'm not sure what he meant by concrete evidence. What shall we do?" asked a dejected Dora.

"I guess we will always have to live in fear in OZ," replied Howard.

"And we will just continue to be mindless robots," added Cher.

"Looks like we will never know what doing the right things feels like," returned Tim.

"Professor Marv will be so disappointed," said Dora.

As Rainbo jumped into Dora's lap, her briefcase slipped to the ground, and from it emerged Eve's laptop. Suddenly, a glimmer of hope reappeared on Dora's face.

"Perhaps, all is not lost!" Dora exclaimed.

Chapter 14 - Marvelous Leadership Secrets

☐ **62.** Remember that leaders work equally well with people at all levels.

☐ **63.** Eliminate fear and manipulation, as these may produce short-term results and harm long-term success.

☐ **64.** Adapt and transform with agility in response to changing environment.

☐ **65.** Embrace diversity of ideas and people as a source of competitive advantage.

☐ **66.** Assess the compatibility of organizational cultures when merging different entities.

Chapter 15: Sustained Integrity Under Duress

A leader is a dealer in hope.
— Napoleon Bonaparte

Dora's mind was whirling around in circles. It was not in her character to disparage anyone, but she had found pieces of evidence linking Eve and Mitchell's involvement to specific instances of organizational misdeeds. Combing the data on Eve's laptop had shown her a hairy mess in the Human Resources and Finance organizations at OZ.

It looked like certain vendors had been awarded untendered contracts year after year despite poor performance and against the appeals of organizational managers. There was reason to suspect that Eve and Mitchell were receiving kickbacks from these vendors. Two employees who had raised serious concerns regarding their practices were issued written warnings to "limit themselves to their assigned jobs," and were later fired on the pretext of performance issues.

The annual Organizational Health Survey results were published selectively. All the concerns raised about the human resource policies were somehow omitted from the results. Even though the surveys were purported to be anonymous, there was evidence that the names of the providers of the negative feedback were sought out from the database and those individuals were targeted for punishment. During restructuring activities, these individuals were mysteriously demoted or forced to leave the company against the protests of their managers.

It appeared that OZ was not generating enough cash and Mitchell's Finance department was using undocumented borrowing to keep the profits high enough to keep the investors unwary. Such artificially boosted profits with a variety of accounting tricks were increasing pressure on the company and setting up OZ for failure in the long term.

Eve and Mitchell traveled extensively at the company's expense. Because of Glenda's outside preoccupations, they were abusing the latitude given to them and misleading the company. To cover the shortfalls from their lavish spending, it appeared that Mitchell was selling company assets and compensating for the sold assets by raising the goodwill value on the balance sheet. It was just a matter of time before Glenda and OZ investors would discover the company's precarious situation.

Dora was in a serious quandary. What were her options? Provide this information to Glenda and The Wizard? Confront Mitchell with these facts? What was the right thing to do? What would Professor Marv do in this situation? She was pondering her choices when her phone rang. As though there were a telepathic connection between them, it was Professor Marv on the line!

"Hello, Miss Marvelous Traveler," Professor said, bringing a smile to her face. "So, you have been enjoying Ruby City so much that you have forgotten to check in with home?"

"Oh, I miss you all so very dearly," she assured him, "and it is so great to hear your voice again. How are you feeling?"

"I am much better. This old heart has not given up yet. But we miss you and have been worried about you. What's been going on, my dear?"

Unexpectedly Dora felt secure. There was nothing so wrong that Professor Marv could not make better with just his guidance and encouragement. To Dora, Professor Marv was the embodiment of justice, wisdom and leadership.

"Are you sure you want to be bothered with the details?" Dora questioned.

Professor Marv responded reassuringly, "No problem. Go ahead."

Dora recounted the main parts of her trip, including her meeting with Glenda, the details about her three new friends at OZ, the state of business and management at the company, the ultimatum from the OZ investor, *and* her latest findings on Eve's laptop.

"You have experienced a lot in a very short amount of time, Dora. Now I understand why you've been so quiet lately," the Professor said with compassion.

"I have been busy, Professor Marv. Now I'm in this serious dilemma about the potential wickedness I have uncovered in Human Resources and Finance. Just when I was wondering what you would do in this situation, you called," Dora said in a curious tone.

"Dora, I sure could tell you what I would do. However, I am not there in the trenches. You are. You have risen up to many tough challenges in the past and I am confident that you will do so again. Just trust your gut for the right answer and let it guide you. Use your ability to see the whole picture. From what you've told me about Tim's sensitive heart, Cher's brainpower, and Howard's courage, collectively the four of you will be able to solve this dilemma. Keep in view that the future of the people at Marvelous and OZ is in your hands. Decide what is best for everyone. Be confident about achieving that result, because rising to the occasion has never meant so much."

Realizing that the Professor wanted to empower her to complete her own journey and find her own solution, she responded, "Thank you, Professor. Your trust and reinforcement means a lot to me. If we want to develop muscles, we have to do our own lifting. I'll reach out to my friends, and we'll put our collective abilities to work and find our way through this thick forest."

"OK, good luck, and I hope to see you soon," said Professor Marv. After a brief exchange of farewells, the line fell silent.

Dora decided that Mitchell ought to be given a chance to defend himself in light of this evidence. Her hope was that he would see the writing on the wall and decide to get his act together or to gracefully exit OZ. To safeguard the data, she stopped by Cher's office to ask if one of her IT techs could back up the laptop data onto a secure external server for safekeeping. Cher's most diligent employee, Ilyas Ahmed Khan, helped Dora back up her data.

That afternoon Dora and Rainbo met with Mitchell. The air in the conference was filled with tension. Mitchell could not stand to be in the same room with his nemesis but realized that he had to know what cards his adversary held. Wingo accompanied his owner as usual. He seemed particularly fidgety that day as if he too were very restless and worried.

"Mitchell, I have been reviewing the contents of Eve's laptop and have found some information that I would like your thoughts on." Dora went on to share with him all the email exchanges, spreadsheets and documents that she had summarized. The process took less than fifteen minutes.

Mitchell sat across the table without expression, chewing on his cigar. Wingo, sitting on a chair beside Mitchell, listened intently to Dora as if he also understood the seriousness of the situation.

"Nice work of fiction, young lady," retorted Mitchell. "How long have you had that laptop in your possession? I see that you have been making good use of your time in your hotel fabricating all kinds of evidence. But Missy, let me tell you that OZ runs on my command. No one is going to believe that sack of lies you have compiled."

"Mitchell, I am not going to argue. I just thought the right thing to do was to share this information to give you an opportunity to provide an explanation," Dora said with sincerity.

"Explanation? I don't owe any explanations to anyone, especially to you. You can take that data and analyze it 'til you are green in your face. It makes no difference to me. On the contrary, I have compiled enough data on you, Missy, and your 'marvelous' little company, and I have already shared it with The Wizard. You might as well say goodbye to the merger that you've been so looking forward to. Book your return flight back to your dumb little chip factory," Mitchell said dismissively.

"OK Mitchell, we will let things take their course then," said Dora as she carefully packed up her laptop and left the conference room.

Wingo jumped across the table as Mitchell tried to grab him roughly.

"Hey Wingo, come over here," commanded Mitchell.

Wingo stood still on the other side, staring back at Mitchell like an angry child.

Mitchell pulled out his long wooden pencil, and threw it at Wingo, who caught it with his long arms and flung it back at Mitchell, striking him hard on his temple. By the time the shaken and fuming Mitchell could react, Wingo escaped through the conference room window, which backed up to a tall tree.

Finally, Wingo had found the will and courage to break free from the tyranny of his wicked master! It was starting to appear that the freedom of the employees at OZ could not be very far behind...or could it?

Chapter 15 - Marvelous Leadership Secrets

- [ ] **67.** Develop trust to gain employee loyalty.
- [ ] **68.** Use sound ethical practices to create sustainable business value.
- [ ] **69.** Aim for a win-win for all parties in every negotiation.
- [ ] **70.** Cultivate and maintain an optimistic and positive attitude.
- [ ] **71.** Give everyone the first chance to explain before final conclusions are drawn.

THE LEADER OF OZ

Chapter 16: Battling the Wicked Forces

Don't tell people how to do things, tell them what to do and let them surprise you with their results.

— George S. Patton

As the cab drove Dora to an offsite location just a few miles from the OZ campus, Dora was thinking about what Mitchell had said and his disparaging remarks about her fabrication of the stories against him. It disturbed her to have her integrity questioned. Nevertheless, with her ability to see things from others' perspectives, she could imagine why Mitchell may have felt that way about her.

As she walked toward the building, she wasn't sure how to start the meeting with Cher, Howard, and Tim. Before she had reached the lobby entrance, she spotted Tim waving her over to a one of the private cottages to the left of the main building. "We're over here," Tim shouted across the lawn. Dora changed direction and quickly arrived at the cottage. When she entered the room, she couldn't believe her eyes.

Flipcharts covered the walls. There were stacks of books and papers on a small table in the center of the room. Cher was fidgeting with a projector displaying a spreadsheet on the wall from her laptop entitled "OZ, The Next Generation Company."

"Did I get the time wrong for our meeting today?" Dora asked worriedly.

"No," Tim said, "you've got the time right. The three of us decided that we needed to take the bull by the horns and put into action our own leadership skills."

Howard chimed in, "Over the past two weeks we've all felt a change in how we work together and started to understand what's really important to each of us personally and professionally. We had expected you to arrive and just overload us with extra tasks to do on top of our regular jobs. You know... what typically happens when auditors arrive. It's been quite a while since we've had any auditors here. Mitchell and Eve seem to do a great job scaring them away."

Howard continued, "You've inspired all of us and made a difference in each of our lives. If you're representative of the people at Marvelous Snacks, we'd like to have a dozen more of you poking around here. So the three of us felt empowered and collectively decided to arrive here early this morning to get started. We thought you'd like to see OZ's future through our perspectives. Our hope was that we could give you something in return to save you time with your analysis and recommendation. This might be the chance to make the merger happen between Marvelous and OZ."

Dora was stunned and somewhat overwhelmed by the expression of support by people that she had only known for two week.

Howard approached Dora and placed his hand on her shoulder. "I'm not sure what you are thinking, but I am sure you can see there's something missing." Dora didn't catch Howard's drift as her confused look tipped off Howard.

"Mitchell," said Howard.

"We've learned from you that we need to work together as a team and put aside our differences. Therefore, we invited Mitchell to be a part of our OZ discussion, Cher said with a serious smile.

Dora's heart skipped a beat. "So is Mitchell here?" she asked nervously.

"No, not yet," said Cher. "He told us he had to conjure up something important this morning to give to Glenda, so he couldn't meet with us before 1:00 PM. He should be here any moment. We've been keeping him in the loop by emailing him our documents over the past few hours."

Retaining her composure, Dora said, "I can't wait to see what you've come up with. This could save me lots of long evening hours preparing for our meeting with Glenda and Professor Marv. Can I quickly see what The Next Generation looks like before Mitchell arrives so that I can be up to speed as well?"

The team of three began to present the well thought-out analysis and plans for how OZ could help Marvelous. They listed all of the strengths, weaknesses, opportunities, and threats for the merger. For each of their departments, they had detailed plans laid out, with recommended timetables and responsibilities.

Dora was impressed, she knew that each of them was a well-respected manager, but collectively they had demonstrated leadership that would have even impressed Professor Marv. Before Dora could see the final elements of the proposal, the door swung open and there stood Mitchell. Wingo, his constant companion, was conspicuously absent.

As Mitchell entered the room, his three peers welcomed him in a way uncharacteristic of the behaviors Dora had seen over the past two weeks. Mitchell walked in front of the projector and all of the data was strewn across his stark white shirt.

He immediately addressed the group, "I had a chance to review what you've been sending me, and it was very helpful for what I was putting together this morning. I'd like to say thank you for the work you've done, but I can't. You don't have enough inside information about OZ to even begin to understand whether your ideas have a prayer in hell of working. This whole idea of thinking that by putting your heads together you could make a difference was just too humorous for me to even put a stop to your wasted effort. The email updates you sent me over the past several hours have kept me well entertained. I can at least thank you for that."

Mitchell pulled the plug on the projector. "Let me save you any additional useless work. I've taken the opportunity to put together my own plan, one that makes good bottom line sense with none of this touchy-feely crap, and sent it to The Wizard. I've already received this email back from him just before I left my office."

With that, Mitchell tossed the email on to the small table and said, "You losers, enjoy the rest of your meeting, I'm heading back to OZ to make plans for the real next generation." With that concluding statement, Mitchell exited the room, slamming the door behind him.

Tim immediately picked up The Wizard's email that Mitchell had left on the table and began to read it aloud. "Mitchell, I have reviewed your new plan for OZ, and the dollars are in line with my expectations. I will contact Glenda to tell her how I want to proceed. No additional work is needed from your side."

Dora and the team were left speechless. Their rollercoaster ride had taken yet another stomach-churning dive into the unknown.

Chapter 16 - Marvelous Leadership Secrets

- [ ] **72.** Deliver superior solutions through collaboration and collective intelligence.
- [ ] **73.** Empower people to assume risk and take initiative.
- [ ] **74.** Inspire people to dream beyond their current reality.
- [ ] **75.** Make a positive difference in people's lives.
- [ ] **76.** Understand who are your allies and adversaries.

THE LEADER OF OZ

Chapter 17: Preparing to Return to OZ

Becoming a leader is synonymous with becoming yourself. It is precisely that simple, and it is also that difficult.

– Warren H. Bennis

The overnight rains left the entire city drenched and gloomy. Amid the turmoil of activities and emotions surrounding the merger, Glenda felt it necessary to provide an appropriate perspective to her staff. Therefore she summoned Mitchell, Cher, Tim and Howard to a special meeting. She also invited Dora as an attendee. Once the entire team arrived, Glenda rose and addressed the meeting with a friendly tenderness in her voice.

"I haven't had a proper chance to share my personal perspectives with you on the merger and its implications, so I thought of calling this meeting with you. Thank you for being here on short notice.

"The transformational change that we seek at OZ is possible, but it will not be easy. It is a long path laced with many obstacles, and the rewards will not come quickly. During this process of change, there will certainly be times when we may wind up feeling worse than we did before we started, but remember that positive results for a better future are only possible with change.

"We have just taken the first few strides in the evaluation process. As tough as these may have seemed, there will be several more challenges that will take creativity and effort from everyone at all levels. Nevertheless, remember that challenges and opportunities are two inseparable associates. When one shows up, the other invariably presents itself.

Anyone remember how the bottled water industry first got started? The engineers were facing a monumental challenge on a subway project. The tunnels they were constructing kept getting filled with water. This presented a heartbreakingly tough challenge. It was not until a maintenance worker discovered how great the tunnel water tasted and brought it to the attention of his supervisor. The water was highly mineralized and had a great taste, so they decided to bottle it for distribution, turning their big challenge into a major opportunity. This spawned a completely new industry for the world. Do you see the inseparability of challenge and opportunity? OZ's future needs exactly this type of courage and creative spirit to find opportunities in our challenges."

Hinting at what transpired at their meeting with The Wizard, Glenda continued, "Success must be viewed holistically. It cannot simply be about costs and benefits, sales and revenues, productivity and efficiency, *or* profits and bonuses. Success has to be viewed in terms of the whole experience and how it impacts the lives, inspiration, belief, and fulfillment of *all* the stakeholders."

Mitchell gulped, as he knew the comment was intended for him, and his face turned a dark shade of crimson.

Glenda continued, "As leaders, we are responsible for creating this total experience for our people. Listening to people is not just important, it is an imperative! Keep in mind that they watch our backs. If we don't pay attention to them, forces invisible to us could strike us down. In this process however, there *is* place for different personalities with diverse perspectives. We are much better off with all kinds of diversity than we are without it.

"One last observation and I will let you all go. Our future at this point depends on our ability to learn and adapt to a new direction. Defensiveness will slow down our response to change on the path of advancement. Rivers flow in only one direction. It is not possible to make them flow in the opposite direction. Let's move with our natural flow and do what we need to do to achieve a great future for all of our people."

Dora, Cher, Tim and Howard received Glenda's points clearly. It was a hopeful and inspirational message with no hint of blame.

Dora's conscience was clear, and she desperately hoped that Mitchell would come clean. Then they could move forward to do what was best for the company and their people although Glenda provided no clue as to the resolution she had in mind.

Mitchell remained quiet but visibly defiant during Glenda's address. It appeared that he was beginning to recognize the cautionary signs. He could feel his power empire at OZ slowly but certainly crumbling like a sand palace under the force of tidal waters. His last hope was The Wizard to whom he had provided his financial analysis arguing in dollars and cents what a big disaster the merger would be. In the face of the evidence discovered by Dora, Mitchell knew his chances of survival could be in question.

For Mitchell, everything now depended on The Wizard. Would he withdraw funding making OZ go bankrupt? What message would Glenda have for Mitchell? Would The Wizard agree to the merger or reject it? Who would stay and who would leave? The next few hours would hold the answers to all these questions.

Chapter 17 - Marvelous Leadership Secrets

☐ **77.** Realize that obstacles lace the path of transformational change and results are not quickly achieved.

☐ **78.** View success in terms of the whole experience and how it impacts people's sense of fulfillment.

☐ **79.** Distinguish and embrace the opportunities that come cloaked as tough challenges.

☐ **80.** Avoid defensiveness, as it slows down the response to needed change.

☐ **81.** Listen to and act upon what you are hearing from people at all levels.

Chapter 18: Recovering After the Meltdown

Partnership acknowledges that we are capable of defining for ourselves the rules and yardsticks by which we live and work.

– Peter Block

Dora spent the entire night thinking about what-if scenarios. She had not informed Glenda of any of the financial and ethical issues that she discovered on Eve's laptop. She was in a quandary. Dora had sent Professor Marv an email and left him a voice message, but she had received no response in more than 24 hours. This delay was unusual because The Professor was always prompt and attentive to Dora's messages. She hoped and prayed that he hadn't experienced a relapse from his heart condition.

Dora entered the OZ lobby that morning still undecided about her next plan of action. She got a double shot espresso coffee in the café to jumpstart her sleep deprived body and fatigued mind. As she sat in the café, she caught a glimpse of Glenda and Mitchell getting into the main lobby elevator. Dora still hoped that Mitchell would come clean with Glenda. She was scheduled to meet with Glenda in fifteen minutes.

Dora sat quietly in the cafeteria pondering various questions. How was the Professor? How disappointed would he be to see all the work that she had done shot down by Mitchell's bottom line-based OZ proposal to The Wizard? What would happen to Glenda, Cher, Tim and Howard? In addition, how would she answer all the questions back at Marvelous about her trip for the last three weeks? Dora could feel herself being sucked into a downward spiral. As she looked up, there stood Cher, Tim and Howard.

They were all smiling at her. Cher handed her another espresso "I can see yours is empty, you'll probably need another, and we're all on our seconds," Cher said with a big smile. Actually, they all were smiling. Did they know something Dora didn't?

"Why are you all smiling? After yesterday's meeting I'd expect the train's arrival to Smileville wouldn't be for quite a while."

Howard responded, "Yea, we all felt pretty depressed. However, over the last two and a half weeks, we've done some of the best work that we've ever done, and last evening we decided that we felt darn good about what we've accomplished. We told you yesterday how empowered we felt and what a difference you made in our lives. We called Glenda last night and asked her if the three of us could stop by and see her at her house."

Cher was smiling and said, "Not sure we used our brains to make that decision... "

Tim continued, "But, we listened to our hearts and the decision was easy."

Howard finalized the statements with "And the three of us did it with courage"

"We showed Glenda all the details on our version of OZ, The Next Generation Company. We also told her that we had invited Mitchell to be a part of it and felt betrayed when he took our ideas and

114

manipulated them into his plan that he gave to The Wizard," Cher said disappointedly.

"Not very ethical and not helpful at all to building a strong team," Tim quickly added. "And finally, we all felt it wasn't very fair to you to have OZ's image tainted by someone such as Witchell. So Glenda told us that the first thing this morning she was going to confront Mitchell and get to the bottom of all of this covert activity."

Holding his espresso high in the air, Howard said, "We all left Glenda's house just after midnight. I've never felt so jazzed by fearlessly walking the leadership walk instead of just talking the talk or diverting the hard discussions to someone else. It finally clicked for me—you have to stand up for what you believe in, no matter what the consequences. And if you lose, you can still look at yourself in the mirror the next day knowing that you did the right thing and retained your integrity."

With that, Cher, Tim and Dora raised their coffee cups and tapped them on Howard's.

"One question for you, Dora," said Howard.

"Sure, what is it?" Dora asked with a smile.

"If the Wizard doesn't like our ideas... well, do you think that you'll have any openings at Marvelous for a few new managers?"

Tim and Cher laughed, but Dora knew there was an ounce of truth in his question.

Looking at her watch, Dora noticed that it was later than she thought, "I've got a meeting with Glenda in two minutes, got to run. Keep up the good

Karma. That's what you Californians say, right?" Dora said, as she collected her things.

They all chuckled and repeated together, "Good Karma!"

As Dora approached Glenda's office, she passed Mitchell in the hallway. There was no exchange of words, just a piercing momentary sinister glance from him. He brushed by Dora as he headed to the open elevator.

Glenda looked distraught when Dora entered her office. "Ten o'clock, you're prompt as always. Please close the door and have a seat," Glenda said in a solemn tone. This was the first time that she had seen Glenda have a closed-door meeting.

Glenda sat down behind her desk and began to speak. "I had a disturbing meeting with Mitchell to discuss ideas for our next steps. After prompting from your three amigos that showed up at my home last night, I called an urgent meeting with Mitchell early this morning."

"I had intended to have a discussion with him about his OZ proposal, which he sent to the Wizard, but the conversation took a strange twist in direction. Before I could say anything, Mitchell closed the door and said, 'I heard you met with Dora yesterday. I am sure she told you a bucketful of lies about what she has been entering into Eve's laptop to discredit me so the merger will go through regardless of my input.'"

"At that point, I was a bit stunned. Dora, I did not know anything about it from you, so I said, 'Mitchell, I'd like to hear your side of the story.' After about 30 minutes of his ranting and raving, I could tell that he was worried, and that the little stunt sending his OZ proposal to The Wizard without my seeing it first was on the side of insubordination. It's a primal reaction when an animal sees itself as preyed upon with no way out. Mitchell is a good accountant, and despite the opportunity I provided him to manage Human Resources, he seems unwilling and unable to learn that there is more to business than numbers."

Taking a deep breath Glenda continued, "Mitchell manages bonus to bonus. There isn't a single part of his brain that thinks long-term. He is the first to try to sacrifice headcount to get short-term profits. Fortunately, I get the final say in those matters. Since I've been too preoccupied with keeping the investors and Wall Street happy over the past year, I'll be the first to admit that I've taken my eye off the ball.

"Ever since I announced the Letter of Intent with my staff, this potential merger with Marvelous has had Mitchell scurrying around like a crazed creature. With the tragedy of losing Eve and his taking on HR responsibilities as well as Finance, I chalked up his recent behavior to stress. Nevertheless, a few red flags popped up for me this past week.

"Yesterday before I arrived at your offsite meeting, I found the truth from our IT Department about many of the so-called lies, which Mitchell had told me you were fabricating. We have a connected data backup for all of our PCs and laptops and strive to maintain the highest integrity, so no one gets to see anyone else's data. With Eve's passing, I personally asked our IT group to canvas her backup files to make sure we had all the HR files we needed. They found some questionable outside correspondence that also had Mitchell's name attached, so I asked them to do some investigating.

"I gave Mitchell just enough rope to hang himself in our meeting this morning. Once he had finished his 30-minutes of non-stop rambling, I let him know that we had already checked the files on Eve's IT backup. Also that you would not have been able to fabricate any lies. At that point, I asked Mitchell to leave his laptop with me and to depart the building. He wasn't happy, but he's smart enough to know when to stop the charade."

Dora felt vindicated. "I can't tell you how relieved I am not to have to share my findings with you on this matter. It is a bit awkward being an outsider, feeling like an internal spy. I had my conversation on the findings only with Mitchell, no one else knows," Dora said sincerely.

Glenda said, "I'll be the bearer of the bad news to the rest of the staff. Thanks for maintaining confidentiality and retaining concern for Finance and HR, even though Mitchell disgraced his responsibility to the company."

"Speaking of bad news: What about Mitchell's OZ proposal to the Wizard?" Dora asked in a concerned voice.

Glenda responded, "That *is* a problem. I've looked at his proposal, and it doesn't include any merger with Marvelous. It is a financial proposal to re-ignite OZ's sales and profitability. However, in true Mitchell fashion, it is myopic. We'd look good initially, but would be in a worse situation than we are in right now in 18 months. But he would have made his bonuses two-fold.

"We'd be into an even deeper hole, which we couldn't get out of. Moreover, as far as the well-being of the OZ employees, that would be questionable. At some point, you just can't squeeze any more productivity out of a person working in an optimized process. Our people are our only competitive advantage since they are the ones that hold the intellectual property. Without them, we're just white buildings with emerald stripes."

"So what happens tomorrow on the call with The Wizard?" Dora asked with serious anticipation.

"I've sent the staff's version of "OZ, The Next Generation" to The Wizard, and I'm expecting you to be there on the 11:00 AM conference call to answer any of the questions he has about what you've concluded regarding the merger. Let's you and I meet in my conference room at 9:00 AM tomorrow for any last minute thoughts and discussions."

"I'll be there," committed Dora.

Chapter 18 - Marvelous Leadership Secrets

☐ **82.** Refrain from viewing leadership as a passive activity.

☐ **83.** Maintain your convictions grounded upon high moral values.

☐ **84.** Role model integrity, as it defines who you are.

☐ **85.** Effectively manage knowledge to secure a competitive advantage.

☐ **86.** Always give a person the first chance to own their success or failure.

Chapter 19: The Wizard Replies

Leaders who ask for input from key stakeholders; learn with a positive, non-defensive attitude; and follow up in a focused, efficient manner will almost invariably grow and develop in terms of increased effectiveness.

— Marshall Goldsmith

Dora returned to her hotel room that evening and flipped open her laptop to prepare for the following morning's meetings with Glenda and The Wizard. She had done her homework over the past weeks and felt that she had a good grasp of OZ's culture, human capital capabilities, financial condition, and synergies with Marvelous. Now all she had to do was put it in a document to review with Glenda in the morning so they could present their findings to The Wizard.

Looking over at Rainbo snuggled up in one of bed pillows she said, "Looks like this will be one of those all-nighters, but it's my last chance to pull it all together for Glenda, The Wizard and Professor Marv. I'm worried about The Professor and I would really like to talk to him for some of his great coaching before my meetings tomorrow." Then she plunged into thinking through the details of the presentation.

Feeling a tug and playful snarl from Rainbo on her pants leg, Dora awoke from a deep sleep. "Oh my!" she exclaimed as she looked at the clock on the desk of her hotel room. "It's 8:00 AM, I must have fallen asleep. I've got a meeting with Glenda at

9:00 AM." Dora jumped out of the desk chair and frantically got herself ready to get over to OZ.

"Ten minutes to spare," Dora said to her perky, panting pet who was sitting on the car seat when they pulled into the OZ parking lot. Dora quickly arrived at Glenda's empty conference room. "Looks like we made it, Rainbo," Dora said with a satisfied smile. She opened her laptop, sent the documents which she had prepared the night before over to the conference room's printer and began arranging them when Glenda walked in.

"I can see that you are already busy and it looks like you have some interesting findings to show me," Glenda said as she gazed at the charts and graphs Dora had spread out on the conference room table before she could finish organizing them.

"I hope so. I spent most of the night on them, until I feel asleep at my laptop," Dora retorted as she tried to cover up her yawning.

"Professor Marv told me you were a very hard worker, and you would leave no stone unturned. By the way, any word from The Professor?" Glenda asked with a hopeful tone.

"No return calls or even an email. I hope that he is OK. I wanted to review my findings with him and get some of his expert coaching, but it looks like I am flying solo this time," Dora sighed.

"Let's hope for the best; no news may be good news," Glenda said in a comforting tone.

Dora and Glenda sat down at the conference table to get ready for the next several hours of discussion before the phone call with The Wizard at noon. Dora started the conversation, "Glenda, first I want to thank you for your support from all of your staff members over the past several weeks. Having their help and the access to the OZ history, files, and information on Eve's laptop has made my job significantly easier that I thought it would be. I didn't really know what to expect, but knowing that you were a close friend of The Professor's, I shouldn't have expected anything less.

"What I propose is that I give you a quick overview of my findings and my recommendation on whether or not we should proceed with the merger, so that I can get your immediate thoughts," Dora said. Pointing to the mound of paper that she had printed before Glenda's arrival, Dora added, "I've got lots of backup, so that we can dive into any of the details that you would like."

Glenda looked impressed, and Dora could see her eagerness to begin the discussion.

Dora quickly began, "I've laid out my summary using a SWOT analysis: Strengths, Weaknesses, Opportunities, and Threats. Your first strength is your People! They are creative, smart, hardworking, open to new ideas, and willing to work together as a team. Your second strength is your product. The OZ product is good, and what I have seen from OZ 2.0, the next generation should be *the* premier tool for anyone doing online business."

Glenda smiled.

"As for the Weaknesses, I have found a few, they are small, but some are more critical to your success than others. Most of them are ones that I believe exist in every company. However, the degree of each differentiates good companies from great ones. The small weaknesses such as resource allocations, department communications, budgeting, and planning can all be turned into strengths through the use of some good training, utilizing new tools, simple process implementations, and just plain diligence. The larger weaknesses are in some of the antiquated and unfunded infrastructures and the lack of consistent alignment with OZ's mission and vision across departments.

"In the Opportunities area, the foundational processes are sound, there is a significant chance to exceed your customer's expectations, develop new customer relationships, and expand into new markets. Getting all departments to work together as a single cohesive unit should improve just about every aspect of OZ's business. In addition, the chance for a merger is an opportunity that could be beneficial for OZ and Marvelous.

"Finally, the Threats: Let's start with Mitchell. The rest of your staff are all team players and have the best of intentions. Mitchell may be a skillful finance person, but I can't see his skills offsetting the amount of fear and havoc he wreaks on your staff members. The values and culture espoused here aren't lived behind the closed office and conference room doors. The more global threat is the chance for your competitors to swoop down and take your entire market share with marginally better software and support appears to be a closer threat than you may think. All of the survival tactics and focus on doing tasks instead of completing deliverables that I have seen in every department is slowing killing your most valuable assets, your people. This unproductive practice is keeping them from focusing on what is most important—the customer."

Glenda didn't appear to disagree with what Dora had just said, but she remained silent. After a few moments, Glenda spoke "You've concisely summed up what I've been feeling over the past year. It's not as if I don't know, but when it is equally as apparent to others, it's a good wakeup call although a hard pill to swallow. Thank you for the level of completeness, honesty, and directness. Regarding some of these significant issues I suppose that I can guess what your recommendation will be for the merger."

Before Dora could respond, there was a light knock on the door. Glenda's assistant entered and handing her a printed email note said, "Sorry to interrupt, but I thought you would want to see this email from The Wizard."

Glenda read the email to Dora, "Glenda, I am canceling our teleconference today. I've reviewed all of materials that Mitchell sent me. I'll let you know my decision tomorrow."

Dora couldn't believe her ears. How could The Wizard make a decision without seeing all of the information? She had worked incredibly hard over the past several weeks, and now it looked like all of her diligence would go to waste.

Seeing Dora's astonishment, Glenda spoke in a comforting tone, "I can see that you are disappointed. Let me sift through the detail of the rest of the documents you have prepared. It sounds like The Wizard may have already made up his mind, but I won't go down without a fight. I'll send all of your information over to The Wizard this afternoon with a note that I concur with your report."

"Thanks for the comforting words," Dora said in a dejected tone as she picked up her briefcase, and headed for the door.

"Dora wait a minute; you were about to tell me your recommendation," Glenda said as she pulled out the folded slip of paper Dora had handed her a week ago. "I am eager to see your ALAS score so that I can see how OZ stacks up to Marvelous' pre-expansion score and if you place some hope for the merger."

Dora pulled the summary page from the document mound in front of Glenda. "Here is the score you've been waiting for," she said, circling the score in red. You'll find everything in the documents. Dora headed toward the door and said, "Glenda, I really need some space this very moment. I'll be back to see you and hear The Wizard's decision tomorrow morning before my 1:00 PM flight. You can reach me today on my cell phone for anything urgent."

With that closing statement and a deflated spirit, Dora walked down the hallway with Rainbo following closely behind.

Chapter 19 - Marvelous Leadership Secrets

- [ ] **87.** Be direct without being abrasive.
- [ ] **88.** Do your homework; let the facts speak for themselves.
- [ ] **89.** Do not underrate the value of persistence.
- [ ] **90.** Know and acknowledge your Strengths, Weaknesses, Opportunities, and Threats.

THE LEADER OF OZ

Chapter 20: Getting Back to Kansas

The "how to be" leader builds dispersed and diverse leadership—distributing leadership to the outermost edges of the circle to unleash the power of shared responsibility.

– Frances Hesselbein

Dora awoke at bit groggy at 10:00 AM. As she turned on her cell phone, she saw several missed calls. She could see that one was The Professor's cell phone, and the rest were from a phone number at OZ, but no voicemails. Excited that the short period of silence with The Professor had ended, she quickly returned the call, but unfortunately, it went directly to his voicemail. She spoke, "Professor, its Dora. I saw that I missed your call from late last night. Please call back, I want to talk to you. I'll be flying back to Kansas this afternoon; I can't wait to get home." With that, she ended the call.

Dora packed her things and did one last check around the hotel room before she and Rainbo headed to the front desk to check out. The two companions departed for their last trip to OZ.

Since her meeting with Glenda on the previous day, Dora had time to mentally recap everything that she had experienced over the last several weeks. She was exhausted and still grappling with the uncertainty of success, concerned how The Professor would react to her findings. Actually, it may be a moot point if The Wizard's decision was the one she thought it would be, based on what Witchell had sent him. "I suppose

I'll know shortly," she thought as she and Rainbo entered the OZ building.

"I'll be sad to say goodbye to all of my new friends here at OZ. I feel like I may have let them down. I arrived with such high hopes and now I could be leaving them on a discouraging note. The Professor always said, 'Leave everything you touch better than you found it' and I do feel everything I've done will leave Cher, Tim, Howard and Glenda with a greater chance of success, regardless of whether or not they merge with Marvelous.'

As she entered the building, Dora heard her name being called while she was headed toward the café for a cup of coffee. "Ms. Dora," the receptionist, Candi Washington, called out, "Glenda and her staff have been trying to reach you all morning. I have a note here for you."

Dora opened the sealed envelope and read, "Please stop by my office immediately when you arrive, the verdict from The Wizard is in — Glenda."

With great anticipation, Dora quickly shifted her route from the café to the elevator and straight to Glenda's office. As she walked down what felt like an endless hallway, she had mixed emotions about hearing the verdict. However, as she entered Glenda's office her emotions quickly shifted when she was greeted by a strong familiar male voice.

"Hi, Dora!" It was Professor Marv! He gave her a big bear hug.

Completely flustered, emotions overwhelmed her as she started her rapid-fire questions. "How are you? Are you all recovered? Did you get my voicemail? What are you doing here?"

"Good. Yes. No. And to see you and Glenda," The Professor shot back at Dora. He still had his good sense of humor, which always brought a smile to others' faces.

"I'm doing fine and I feel much better. My heart was sending me a message but the doctor said there was no permanent damage. He started me on a new lifestyle and, if I follow his prescription, I'll be in good health for another thirty years."

"I ran over here from the hotel early this morning to see you and Glenda, and I do mean ran," The Professor concluded, looking proud.

Dora couldn't have been happier or more relieved. Rainbo looked equally as pleased as he jumped into The Professor's lap to greet him.

Another rush of emotions came over Dora as she began to speak, "Glenda, I got your urgent message from the receptionist that you've received the verdict from The Wizard."

"Dora, please sit down, I thought I'd let The Wizard tell you the verdict himself," Glenda said almost cheerfully.

Dora expected Glenda to punch in a phone number on the conference phone sitting on the desk in front of them; instead, she turned to The Professor.

The Professor said confidently with a smile, "We're moving forward with the merger."

Confused, by The Professor's statement Dora inquired, "Did you talk to The Wizard?" Glenda and

Professor Marv both smiled and laughed, confusing Dora even more.

The Professor leaned across the table to get closer to Dora "I spoke to The Wizard, in a manner of speaking. Dora, I am Wizir, The Wizard!"

Dora dropped back in her chair and, in an even more confused voice, said, "I don't understand."

Glenda broke into the conversation, "When I first started OZ and was struggling to keep it going, Marv gave me the venture capital to get us to where we are today. He did it with one stipulation, that he would remain an anonymous investor. Therefore, I used Marv's high school nickname: Wizir. We wanted our business relationship to be strictly professional and not to be viewed as a favor for a friend."

The Professor continued the conversation, "Actually I've been quietly investing my own good fortune that I made from the success at Marvelous in leaders such as Glenda for more than twenty years. You know I've always believed that giving back to others has its own rewards. I make my investment decisions on people first and then on financials. People that have great leadership potential can do almost anything. Glenda is proof of that, and I am glad to be a part of her success. Through the merger, our success and OZ's success will be one and the same."

Dora was starting to see all of the pieces fitting together. Nevertheless, she still had a few unanswered questions. "Why send me here to do the evaluation? And why didn't you tell me all of this information before I left Farmden?" Dora asked slowly.

Professor Marv responded, "I needed you to be completely unbiased in your assessment. I truly wanted to stretch your talent for problem solving and observation to the next level. I felt it was important for you to do it on your own without my help. My short trip to the hospital made sure that I'd keep my fingers out of the cookie jar." He face reflected his good humor as he said, "Remember, I know how you love a challenge!"

Dora continued the conversation, "Thank you for your confidence in me, I do love a challenge, but I would have appreciated a little less stretching. You said that the merger is moving forward and I haven't even had a chance to show you my findings and give you my recommendation."

The Professor smiled and spoke to Dora, "I arrived here at OZ yesterday afternoon, apparently shortly after you left. Glenda said that you told her that you needed some space. She and I spent the rest of the afternoon and most of the evening, sifting through your merger dissertation. I can see that you've done some great work here," as The Professor pointed to the large pile of documents Dora had left for Glenda the previous day.

Glenda pulled out of her purse the folded slip of paper that Dora had given her on the first day she arrived at OZ and handed it to The Professor. Unfolding the paper, he could see "55" written on it.

"With an ALAS score for OZ even better than the starting point Marvelous had when The Mayor came in to help with our first expansion, I concur with the conclusion you had written to move forward with the merger. Are there any more questions?" The Professor said with confidence.

"Just one more question: What about all the information that Mitchell had sent to The Wizard... I mean to you?" Dora asked with anticipation.

Becoming serious again, The Professor responded, "Glenda has been concerned about his behavior and practices ever since he moved into his current position. Mitchell didn't understand my relationship with Glenda and with the good people at OZ. He had a meltdown in the office yesterday morning when Glenda gave him his walking papers." With this statement, the meeting between the three ended and The Professor asked Dora to continue with her travel plans back to Kansas.

"Hail, Dora!" three voices sang out in unison. Cher, Tim and Howard appeared in the doorway. "You've done it! Witchell is *out*, and the merger is *in*." Howard said with the utmost pride. Glenda continued, "We tried several times to get a hold of you on your cell phone this morning, but were unable to reach you. I wanted you to be at the emergency staff meeting I called this morning for the merger announcement."

"We're all going to be sorry to see you go, but with the merger we're confident that we'll get to see you again," Cher said as they all hugged Dora.

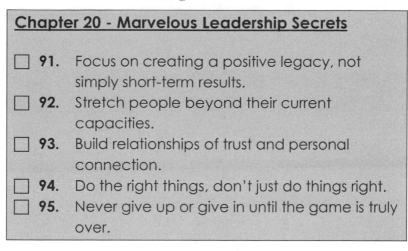

Chapter 20 - Marvelous Leadership Secrets

- [ ] **91.** Focus on creating a positive legacy, not simply short-term results.
- [ ] **92.** Stretch people beyond their current capacities.
- [ ] **93.** Build relationships of trust and personal connection.
- [ ] **94.** Do the right things, don't just do things right.
- [ ] **95.** Never give up or give in until the game is truly over.

THE LEADER OF OZ

Chapter 21: There's Still No Place Like Home

The challenges of systemic change...will require
a unique mix of different people, in different
positions, who lead in different ways.
— Peter M. Senge

The singing of the bluebirds and the gentle tapping of the rain on Dora's tin porch roof woke her out of her sleep. She had not slept this peacefully in three weeks. The sleep worked like a magic elixir to heal her tired mind and strained body. Her plane had landed in Kansas at 9:30 PM the previous night. She was back at her home sweet home once again!

As her bedside clock displayed 6:00 AM in bright red numbers, Dora got out of bed and walked across the room to the small dog bed. Rainbo lay there amusing himself with his chew toy. He sprang up as soon as he saw Dora. The two friends stepped outside to have fun in the mild drizzle of rain. Oh, how they had missed the sights, scents, and sounds of home!

The whole experience in Ruby City of OZ suddenly seemed very surreal. Although they had just been away for three weeks, it felt as if they had spent an eternity there. Dora already missed Cher, Tim and Howard, as she had developed a deep attachment to them. Dora could not forget the tearful goodbye she had received just prior to her departure. With a yearning heart, she hoped that their paths would cross someday again.

It was now 7:00 AM. The drizzle stopped and sunlight started shining brilliantly into Dora's room through the gaps in the clouds. Getting ready to leave for work, her heart rejoiced at the thought that she would once again be reunited with her beloved friends and colleagues at Marvelous Snacks. Rainbo looked as proud as a new freshman going back to school after a long summer break. Together, they made their way to the Marvelous Snacks' headquarters.

As soon as Dora entered the building, she noticed a prominent banner in the lobby that read:

Special Update Meeting Today at 10:00 AM.

Professor Marv Will Address All Employees.

Everyone Encouraged To Attend.

The receptionist handed Dora a sealed envelope from the Professor. He had also flown back to Kansas! Dora was delighted to see that the Professor would be addressing all the employees, although she was not sure about everything he might be presenting. Just then Zach, Hillary and Hank entered the lobby and saw Dora. Much to the chagrin of the security personnel, they all created a bit of commotion screaming in joy and exchanging warm embraces. They just couldn't help it!

"How have you been, stranger? You must have been very busy in the Ruby City...there were only sketchy reports on how things were going out there," said Hank.

"We missed you every day and were beginning to wonder if you got recruited by some ''City' firm," remarked Hillary jokingly.

"We have heard that people's brains in the Ruby City are so full of bright ideas that radical innovation is just part of a normal working day. Is that true?" asked Zach.

"I'll tell you all about it, once I put my brief case down, take off my jacket, and get a cup of coffee," Dora said with a broad smile.

As they briskly walked to their office area, Hank spotted the banner and said to the others, "Hey, it looks like Professor Marv is back! Woo-hoo!!! Anyone know what this 'Special Update Meeting' is about?"

"I have no idea. I left the building at 10 PM last night and the banner was not there. It must have been put up in the wee hours of the morning. Dora, does it have something to do with your work in Ruby City?" replied Zach.

Just then Dora opened the envelope in confidence and saw that there was a note in it from Professor Marv.

"I'm not quite sure; the Professor hasn't said anything to me. Apparently, from this note, I have a meeting with him at 9:00 AM today, maybe I'll get some more insight then," weighed in Dora.

The friends continued their repartee while Dora gave them a quick overview of her trip. Then she concluded, "If my meeting finishes by then, I'll stop by and we can all walk together to the meeting." Agreeing, they dispersed to their own offices to begin their workday.

Dora's face held a shocked, wondrous look as she left the conference room after her meeting with Professor Marv. She joined her friends as per their plan, and they walked together to the meeting location.

At 10:00 AM sharp Professor Marv arrived on stage looking every bit as dapper as he looked on the day of the last Business Review Meeting. There were, however, subtle signs of physical fatigue aggravated by his rushed trip back from OZ. Even if he was in any pain, Professor Marv was not one to show it to anyone. He appeared to be in very high spirits.

As usual, he received a rousing reception from the employees, many of whom were in tears just to see him for the first time since he had been released from the hospital. They all realized that they could have lost their beloved leader. As he stepped up to the podium, Professor Marv's connection with all his employees was very obvious. His work and personal touch over the past thirty years had created a strong mutual bond.

"Dear friends, welcome to this special meeting. As you know, the last few weeks have been tumultuous. I'd like to thank you all for your good wishes and prayers. I also commend you for keeping your focus on your jobs and on Marvelous Snacks during my absence. If someone wants to see a rainbow, they must be ready to endure the rain. This is true in life *and* in business."

Inviting Dora to the stage with him, the Professor continued, "To ensure that we continue to pass the test of change with flying colors, I had asked Dora to manage a special project on behalf of all of us at Marvelous Snacks. The objective of this project was to prepare our company to thrive in our next stage of business. Based on Dora's findings and my vision of the future, I have made some very crucial decisions, which I wish to share with you today.

"Marvelous Snacks will be merging with OZborn Technology, a company based in Ruby City, California, that will give us the immediate ability to begin distributing our products around the globe using their electronic commerce technology. We have been well known in our market here, but soon we will be world famous. It's time the rest of the hungry people around the world got to enjoy a taste of the Marvelous Snacks experience!"

The crowd reacted with a quiet murmur. Dora's heart fluttered at those words. Her mind was heavy with the responsibility that she owed to everyone at the meeting.

Professor Marv continued, "I believe this merger will make us stronger and prepare us to face the challenges of the future. I want you to know one thing very clearly. This merger will affect no one's job. On the contrary, this merger will enable us to create more opportunities for each one of you to grow and blossom.

"Finally, nature teaches us that in order for new flowers to bloom, the old flowers have to fade away. In keeping with this natural process, it is time for me to make way for new leadership to bloom."

The employees were stunned and began to grumble. Professor Marv quietly signaled them to hold their concerns, as a group of new faces joined him on the stage.

"It is time for us to get new blood flowing through our company's veins." The Professor walked over to the people on the stage. "In connection with this, I have four announcements for our merged company:

Hank Straumann and Cher Crowe will co-lead the Finance and Operations organizations.

Hillary Woodsmith and Tim Mann will co-lead the Design and Manufacturing organizations.

Zach Coward and Howard Lee Lyon will co-lead the Marketing and Sales organizations."

Walking over to Dora, he concluded,

"And finally, Dora Gayle will replace me as the Chief Executive Officer and President of our new company."

The employees all rose from their chairs and gave a long round of applause to the new appointees. Even as there was some commotion due to the significant changes just announced, it was clear that the employees believed in Professor Marv's vision and judgment.

"I trust that you will give your full support to our new leaders as they carry out their responsibilities. By no means will I be completely out of the picture. I will serve as the Chairman of the Board. I encourage each of you to meet with your new management team over the next two hours. They will be here to answer any questions you may have."

Dora was pleasantly surprised to find that Cher, Tim and Howard had flown back with Professor Marv. Rainbo went berserk with happiness at the sight of seeing everyone from OZ. As the managers from both companies spoke, for some strange reason, it seemed as if they had known one another for a very long time.

Dora sincerely thanked Professor Marv for the opportunity, and he remarked, "You are the best person to lead the company because I know that you understand the importance of putting people first in all considerations. Good luck, I will trust your decisions as you assume your new responsibilities."

In a moment of concern, Dora recognized that there was one person conspicuously missing from the event. "But, what about Glenda?" Dora asked.

"Of course, Glenda will be available to help as you begin your new role. Do you remember her sharing that she had been distracted over the past year and not paying enough attention to OZ?" the Professor asked. "She's been finalizing the details to begin a brand new start-up overseas. We will close that deal this week, and she'll move into the leadership position there. It's a great opportunity for her to stretch also. Plus, I have asked her to sit on the board of Marvel-OZ with me," said Professor Marv.

Dora was very pleased and excited about what she just heard. "Oh my, I wish Glenda were here," she said. Just as Dora spoke those words, Glenda emerged from the shadows. Dora was overcome with emotion when she saw her.

"Congratulations, Dora. You are the right person for the job, and I am extremely happy for you. I will be going into an exciting and different world overseas to be a 'guardian angel' for a new group of innovators and entrepreneurs." Dora clearly understood that the future of this great company would now be resting on her shoulders.

With quiet confidence and humility, she greeted each employee and made a promise to herself that she would continue to do everything to serve them to the best of her ability.

Although she had enjoyed Ruby City, Dora whispered to Rainbo, "There's still no place like home!"

Chapter 21 - Marvelous Leadership Secrets

☐ **96.** Appreciate that leadership is a contagious process.

☐ **97.** Reward and recognize people's efforts to make a difference.

☐ **98.** Cultivate people with potential to deliver lasting results.

☐ **99.** Know the importance of succession planning and when to pass on the baton.

☐ **100.** Make mentoring an imperative for developing leadership bench strength.

Your Marvelous Leadership Score

Put the appropriate check ☑ from your chapter scores

Brain (B)	Heart (H)	Nerve (N)	Wisdom (W)
7	10	4	1
9	13	6	2
15	20	8	3
17	29	11	5
24	35	12	16
28	39	14	18
32	44	21	19
34	47	26	22
37	48	31	23
40	52	33	25
49	53	41	27
61	54	42	30
69	57	43	36
71	58	45	38
76	59	46	50
79	60	63	51
80	62	67	55
82	65	73	56
86	68	77	64
87	70	84	66
88	74	89	72
92	75	90	81
96	78	94	85
97	83	95	91
98	93	99	100
B Score =	H Score =	N Score =	W Score =
		Total Score B+H+N+W =	

For more details to help you understand your scores, please go to *www.theleaderofoz.com*.

Marvelous Leadership Secrets

☐ **101.** Apply the 100 secrets of Marvelous
Leadership to create a marvelous place to
work.

Our Leadership Philosophy

We believe that everyone in an organization from Day One should not only be given the opportunity to lead, but also be expected to lead. Organizations can realize their full potential only by tapping into the promise of each and every person. Leading people is not a trivial matter. Leadership is a skill and talent that can be cultivated given the right focus and resources. In our journey across 70 nations we have learned two critically important things about leadership:

1. One size does not fit all. National culture plays a significant role in the level of organizational and business results that can be achieved.
2. Most companies and organizations have the right people. However, people engage in their work at their maximum potential only when their leaders take interest in understanding and accommodating their behaviors, values, and learning styles.

The Leader of OZ presents the 10 dimensions of marvelous leadership:
1) Authenticity, 2) Communication, 3) Competence, 4) Confidence, 5) Creativity, 6) Cultural Leadership, 7) Empowerment, 8) Reinforcement, 9) Stewardship, and 10) Visionary Leadership.

You can request an executive briefing or keynote speech to bring the marvelous leadership secrets of OZ to your organization. Information about our proven management and leadership programs, assessments and solutions are found at www.magnaleadership.com.

-Dr. Kevin D. Gazzara and Dr. Murtuza Ali Lakhani

My Marvelous Leadership Notes

My Marvelous Leadership Notes

My Marvelous Leadership Notes

My Marvelous Leadership Notes

Index